UNSTOPPABLE

THE POWER OF NEVER GIVING UP

JORDAN STEVENSON

Photos by Alexx Davila

Book Design by Golden Lane Publishing

Golden Lane Publishing, LLC

Portland, Oregon

www.goldenlanepublishing.com

For all the physically and mentally wounded service men and women. Those who remain fighting even after the uniform has come off. I dedicate this book to you. I am proud of you. I believe in you. I will always fight beside you.

CONTENTS

INTRODUCTION

Since I got hurt, I have been approached multiple times about the idea of writing this book. People would hear about my story, and they would say I should really write a book or have some way for people to read about the experiences I had gone through. I thought about it. But honestly, the idea of writing a book was too intimidating for a military-enlisted college dropout like me. I started writing on my phone and keeping notes on my computer; a couple of entries are about as far as I got. I even went as far as to speak with a couple different publishers about it, but I never took it too seriously. That all changed on November 18th, 2021, when I got the news that my counterpart during my deployment in Afghanistan, Chief Steve Cooper, had committed suicide. Survivor's guilt is defined as "a condition of persistent mental and emotional

stress experienced by someone who has survived an inci-
dent in which others died," I don't know if my experience
fits the definition, but to me, it sure feels like it. Coop and
I never had the opportunity to reconcile the trauma we
both endured due to my injuries.

As my team leader for that deployment, he assigned me to
mount the wall where I got shot. I'll always wonder if my
injuries had anything to do with his decision. Was there a
phone call I could have made? A phone call to say, "I'm
okay. I'm not mad at you, and I don't blame you." I will
always carry around that guilt, thinking, "I should have
just called him one more time." I'll always wonder if I had
called him if that would have made the difference. Would
he still be here? I'll never know. I don't hold him accountable for what happened to me. I don't know what he
carried with him in the end, but I pray that he didn't carry
any guilt about what happened since he was my boss the
night of my injury. I've never held any ill will towards
him. He was just doing his job, and I see what happened
as the cost of war. It is what it is, and there's nothing we
can do about it.

It was a tough pill to swallow because Cooper was always
looking out for me and giving me guidance, even in death,
and to this day, he is still giving me that guidance. He has
made me realize my recovery is an opportunity to use the

experience to do more. Before, I hadn't considered my story to be anything more than the guy who got shot in the head and survived. I wasn't interested in writing a book. But that all changed when I found out he took his own life. For some reason, it hit me differently. I was devastated. That phone call shook me to my core. The experience of losing Coop really kicked me into gear to be more of an example to those around me. For the first time, I started to think people might look up to me or hear my story and possibly be changed by it. It felt like Coop was there, reminding me that as an Explosive Ordinance Disposal Technician (EOD Tech), it was my job to keep my team safe, and it was time to get back to work. I had always known that the statistics on suicide among veterans were not good. Coop reminded me that I had the ability to actually help people, which moved me to do something while I still can. Even if it helps just one person, it's worth it. I owe it to Coop to at least try. My hope is that maybe I can make some kind of a difference for people like him and people like me. Not to quit, not to give up. To be able to find belief in themself and possibly find me and my story as part of their support network.

I was motivated to reach out to people, those who are struggling and going through things I had already been through. I wanted to be part of the team again. So, if I could find a way to still help the team, I would be extremely proud to do that. Chief Cooper's death motivated me and made me realize if I stepped out of my own way and allowed myself to be vulnerable, I could become a real asset. As I was writing this book, I kept thinking, "I want to change my readers lives." I want to speak to anyone who finds themselves in the same place my friend did and tell them it's okay, life will move on, and through the darkness, there's always hope.

I am writing in honor of Steve Cooper and for anyone struggling to find hope. I know what it's like. I've been down to rock bottom and had to find a way to climb out. I've been lost in the dark and had to create my own light to find a way out. I'm not here to give you a rah-rah speech or the 1-2-3 steps. I'm here to tell you it's possible. The rest is up to you.

Before I tell you some stories about my life, you need to know something about me. First and foremost, I'm a dad. And being a dad is a big part of who I am now. I use the word *now* purposefully; before my injuries, my son and marriage were not the priorities they should have been. Thankfully, in the years following my injury, I've made those changes in my life. Now, not a day goes by when my marriage and my children are not my top priority. And as the saying goes, "Behind, every good man is a better woman." Without my wife, Sarah, none of the changes and progress that I've made would have been possible. From the moment I met Sarah, she saw potential in me that I didn't see in myself. She didn't see all my flaws and past bad decisions. Sarah's responsible for getting me back in the gym and my overall physical and mental recovery. She's loved my son in such a way it showed me how to be a better father. Nearly all the connections and progress I've made in my professional career have come through Sarah and her belief in me.

I'm never particularly eager to brag or talk about myself that much because, from my perspective, I'm no different than anybody else. Most people, including myself, have been through difficult times at one point or another. I've met people from all walks of life who have told me about the tough things they've endured. When your wounds are as visible as mine, people feel safe to share with me what's happened to them. And one thing always stands out. People are impressive. I'm no different than you, your neighbor, or your coworker. I'm just Jordan. I'm just a normal guy who's been through some uniquely difficult things I've had to overcome and get through. Nothing about me makes me any more special or better than you. I just happened to find myself in a unique circumstance, just like you find yourself in your unique circumstances, uniquely difficult to you.

I'm a seven-year combat veteran. I worked in the Special Forces in the United States Navy as an Explosive Ordinance Disposal Technician, or EOD Tech for short. Which is just a fancy way of saying I was part of the Special Forces bomb squad. As an EOD Tech, I was responsible for clearing and making safe all explosives ranging from improvised explosive devices (IEDs), underwater mines, nuclear, chemical, and biological bombs. If it went boom, it was my responsibility.

When I was writing this book, I wanted you to experience all the ups and downs right there with me throughout my recovery; that way, you could see all the incredible highs and the devastating lows that I went through. I've had to recall everything from memory because I didn't have a film crew following me and documenting everything the whole time. What I went through was super traumatic, so when I asked myself to recall how it all went down, I realized there was simply too much to unpack. Anyone who's experienced trauma will tell you the tremendous amount that goes through your mind at every stage of the recovery process. Detailing every moment of this book was just plain unrealistic. So, I decided to create a situation where you, the reader, can experience my life through a collection of snapshots, mini snippets of events, and moments that, as a collective, connect to tell a bigger story.

I hope this format will help you connect and relate to some of the things that happened to me. It might even help you better understand yourself. I believe the only true way to help each other as humans is to share with each other the things that have happened to us. That's how we learn about life. Remember, I'm just a regular guy, sharing stories, talking to you friend to friend.

When people ask me how did you do it? How did you get to where you are? How long have you been in recovery? I tell them I'm still in recovery and will be in recovery for the rest of my life. I don't understand why the word recovery has such a negative connotation. Recovery isn't something to be ashamed of. It should be celebrated. My recovery has been a process of reshaping my mindset to keep me focused on my goals and my future instead of the past. I like to think of goals as ever-changing as I am constantly changing, leading me to redefine what my goals are. That's what you have to do sometimes to keep pushing through even when you hit a new challenge in life.

I didn't want this book to be like any other self-help book. I'm not an expert in giving ways to "follow these steps, and you can be successful." I don't believe success is a one-size-fits-all solution. I believe everyone's steps are different. Your steps in life are entirely different than mine, even though you might find we have things in common. My point is how you walk through life and get through whatever you're going through is ultimately determined by your unique personality and mentality. We move forward by choosing to take those next steps in life. What success looks like is up to the individual. At the end of the day, how you live your life is up to you, and it's your choice. No one else gets to decide.

My goal is by the time you put down my book, you feel empowered, knowing you are strong enough to do the things in front of you. We don't always know what cards life will hand us. If someone had told me what I was about to go through before it happened to me, I don't know if I'd have been confident enough to say I'd make it. The truth is we don't know what tomorrow will bring. What matters is we get to choose how we handle it. Good or bad moving forward is up to you.

PART ONE
MAN DOWN

THE NIGHT OF MY INJURY

December 16, 2011

Afghanistan

I got up early, even though we had an operation the night before. The extreme time change made getting good sleep a challenge. When I couldn't sleep, I was working out in the private gym the Army Rangers had on a separate piece of the compound where we resided. My time working with the Marine Recon guys turned me into a gym rat. I lifted shoulders, climbed on the ladder machine, and did handstand pushups against the wall in the corner. I remember working out so hard to the point of exhaustion, where lifting my arms became hard. Little did I know it would be a long time before I'd step foot into a gym again. I finished up my workout and then got a call.

I met up with the Explosive Ordinance Disposal Chief (EODC), Steve Cooper, to get briefed on that night's operation. Chief Cooper was my team leader, filling me in on all the intel. He told me what we were going to be doing that night and what equipment and weapons I was expected to pack. We were going to assault a house like we did the night before. But this time, we were tasked to extract a high-value target (HVT) from a compound under the cover of darkness. You know how some people in America park their cars in the grass, in their front yard? It was kind of like that. Except, in Afghanistan, they park their cars in yards that are surrounded by giant concrete, dirt walls. And the walls surrounded the entire perimeter of the property.

Chief Cooper said to me, "You're on the ladder. I need you to visually clear the vehicles inside the compound of possible IED threats before our guys go in." This meant that I was going to climb a ladder and look over the wall. The goal was for me to get a visual of what was on the inside of the compound. I was to take a good look at the vehicles and look for cues, like if a vehicle was leaned over more than it should be or weighted down on one side, anything that might cue that it was booby-trapped or ready to explode. If I saw anything that remotely looked like a vehicle-born improvised explosive device (VBIED), that was my cue to signal to Chief Cooper. My job was critical in terms of protecting my team. Since my guys would eventually raid the compound, it was my responsibility to make sure none of the vehicles would explode and kill anyone.

After the briefing, I called my wife at the time, Krista. I remember telling her that I was nervous. I had this uneasy feeling that something was going to go wrong. So, I trusted my gut and took the opportunity to say goodbye. I said, "I love you. Give our son a kiss for me. Hug him and tell him that I miss him and that I can't wait to see him when I get home."

It was the single coldest night of my life. This was a cold I had never felt before. None of the prior nights had ever been this cold. It was painful. The perfect mix of wind and cold penetrated every part of my being and soul. And no matter what I did, I couldn't get warm. Waiting on the tarmac for the helicopter, we froze, trying to rub my hands together and thinking, "These little hand warmers aren't doing shit." I was worried. I thought, "I don't know if I'm going to be able to do my job. Was I going to be able to use my hands?" I needed every ounce of strength I had in my body to climb the ladder and make it to the top. My hands were completely numb, and that didn't make it any easier. I hoped that once my adrenaline started pumping, I would be able to block out the pain of the cold. We could hear the helicopters approaching. Cold or not, it was "go" time.

The blast of wind from the giant CH-47 Chinook felt like knives hitting my anxious body. And as quickly as I got onto the helicopter, we landed. We were far enough from the site that we weren't worried about being detected. But who knows. The sound of the helicopter was unmistakable, especially in the dead silence, in the mountains, in the middle of the night. And before I knew it, we were on the ground, running towards our target.

The ground was some of the roughest terrain I had ever seen, frozen solid. It reminded me of my Grandpa Bert's walnut orchards in Modesto near my home that I grew up around in Elk Grove, California. You know when the farmer's fields are all cleared out? And you can see the ditches made from the plows that ran through the dirt so farmers could plant their crops? That's what it was like, except the ground wasn't soft. It was rock hard, like ice. We kept running.

It was pitch black, and we were using night vision. I remember a junior enlisted guy was assigned to me to carry my ladder. We ran towards the building. As we ran, we went down a ditch and then up to the wall. My guy set up the ladder and held the bottom of it firmly so I could climb to the top. This was the first experience I ever had with this type of assignment, so without thinking about it, I unknowingly silhouetted myself against the moonlight. I should have stayed low and close to the wall, hiding myself, but instead, I peered over the wall, exposing myself as a potential target.

Looking over the wall, it appeared clear to me. None of the vehicles inside the compound gave me any clues of explosives rendered inside. None of it appeared to be alarming. I radioed Chief Cooper to inform him it was clear to move in and follow through with the assault without fearing any VBIED threats. And that's the last thing that I remember.

THE MEDIC'S PERSPECTIVE

December 16, 2011

Afghanistan

Robert Moreno

I looked at the thermometer; it said it was negative 10 degrees. I don't know if it was accurate or not, but I do know it was damn cold. I followed standard procedures, getting ready for the day on a reverse type of schedule. As a medic, I'd prep for the night's operation order first, above anything else. Just as quickly as the sun would rise, the night fell and we were on the helicopter, heading towards our target. We got to the compound. I remember seeing a big gate in front of the target we were facing.

I was with the commander. And that's right around the time when all the personnel, everyone on the team, went off to take their positions to complete their mission tasks. The EOD Technician, Jordan Stevenson, took his position on the ladder, doing his job to ensure there were no booby traps. I watched from a distance. I saw the ladder go up and the other guys on the mission getting into position at the front of the breach. Just a few minutes later, we heard gunshots. Initially, it was just a few quick, short bursts, but then everyone jumped in and opened fire into the compound.

Over the radio, I heard someone was hit and needed the medic. It was time to go to work. I ran up to the left of the breach, where I saw the ladders go up. When I got there, people were on other ladders shooting over the wall. There was a group of guys huddled around someone. I pushed my way through and saw Jordan on the ground. He had gone up the ladder, just doing his job to scope the site for any explosive devices, but I thought he must have exposed himself to the moon illumination. All it took was one guy seeing his silhouette against the moonlight, and he took his opportunity and shot at Jordan. Everyone was trying to figure out what was going on. I told everybody to clear out, and I started looking at Jordan from a glance, looking at him from head to toe.

His eyes were glazed over. I felt underneath his neck, took off his helmet, and saw a pool of blood. My muscle memory kicked into gear. I continued my exam, checking him up and down from head to toe. And that's when I noticed the gunshot wound to his head. That became my focal point. I was surprised that I didn't see any other injuries, considering he fell from the top of a ladder, which must have been at least a 20-foot fall. The team and I pulled him away from the wall, dragged him away from the fight, and towards an embankment. Even though I was trained for this and had seen my fair share of head wounds, this wound was significant and compromised his skull, which was something I had never seen before. The gravity of Jordan's injury and the challenge we were up against started to sink in. I knew we had to get him to the hospital immediately. We were at the bottom of the embankment, in thick brush. In order to get him to the helicopter landing zone (HLZ), we first had to get him on the stretcher and transport him over the thick, frozen terrain. The guys in the platoon were quick with delivering the stretcher. While they worked on getting him strapped in, I worked on pinpointing exactly where the majority of the bleeding was coming from. The amount of blood emerging from Jordan's head was concerning. I paid close attention to his wound while the guys continued to tie his body to the stretcher. The amount of blood loss caused me to use all the gauze that I had. I wiped away as much as I could and stuck just enough gauze into his skull so we could get moving to the HLZ.

I noticed he was in and out and mumbling. I proceeded to ask him questions. "What's your name? Where are you from? Do you know where you're at?" Surprisingly,

Jordan replied, "San Diego." I thought, "Holy shit, this guy has a big hole in his head, and he's still talking!"

I kept asking him more questions as we worked on getting him up and over the hedge. This became my on-going system for assessing Jordan's condition and keeping him with us. The commander and the first sergeant yelled in my ear over the radio for an update. I tuned them out temporarily. I kept loosely wrapping his head with gauze, and every time it became soaked with blood immediately. Once I had control of it, I never let go. The rest of the night, I continued to use one hand to control the bleeding while I did everything else with my other hand.

At one point, he stopped responding verbally. I grabbed his hand with my free hand and yelled in his ear, "Jordan, if you can hear me, squeeze my hand!" Jordan squeezed. The pressure in my hand let me know he was still there. He was fighting. Thank God.

Once I realized he was fighting to stay alive, I knew I needed to relay to the first sergeant and the commander what was happening. The first sergeant came over, saw the blood, and said, "Pack that shit!" I looked at him and said, "Fuck no, get out of here! I'm not going to pack a bunch of gauze into this guy's brain and skull." It was obvious. This was a stressful event. I knew they were just trying to do their jobs. I didn't let it affect my ability to focus and make decisions from a Medic's point of view. And I wasn't about to give Jordan life-long brain damage by stuffing a bunch of unnecessary gauze into his skull.

We could hear helicopters nearby. They heard that the troops were in contact and immediately headed over to the HLZ. It didn't take long for them to arrive. Since Jordan's injury took place just moments after drop-off, they were still close by. We needed more time, so I told the commander to call them off because we weren't ready yet. I knew what I had to do to stabilize Jordan.

Once he was stabilized, I got a group of guys to huddle around, and in unison, we picked up the stretcher together and started running toward the HLZ. It was one of the worst runs ever, running through the snow, over the rough terrain, in the freezing cold. And the whole time while running, I kept one hand on the gauze and used the other hand to maintain communication with Jordan by squeezing his hand. Jordan picked up on what I was trying to do because when I would squeeze his hand, he would squeeze mine.

The rerouting of the helicopters meant more running to a new HLZ. One of the guys yelled, saying they were losing grip and the sides of the stretcher were about to fall.

Which honestly, I don't know how we all didn't fall, but he did, and it dropped. That pissed me off. I yelled at the new HLZ, all while trying to maintain control of his head wound. We finally made it only to find out the helicopter was just a transport, a Chinook, not a Medivac.

So, when we got on the helicopter, it was just me and the crew chief on board. We got on the radio immediately to give the hospital teams advanced notice that we were coming. The flight seemed to take forever. Thankfully, they had enough lights on in the back so I could finally see what I was doing. As soon as we lifted off, I grabbed my aid bag, gave him an IV, and went through the entire protocol.

Every time I thought I had control over the hemorrhage, Jordan would reach up and rip out the entire thing of gauze I had on his head. It just kept happening. I'd pull out another piece of gauze to recover the hemorrhage, and he'd reach up and yank it out again. It was back and forth, and annoying but at least it was a useful tool to let me know he was still kind of with it.

I started an IV and tried to get him warm. It was freezing cold, and he had already lost a lot of blood. And I don't know if it was the elevation, considering we were already at between 7,000 and 9,000 feet. But, when we got in the helicopter and took off, within a few minutes, he completely became unresponsive and started vomiting. I couldn't turn his head that easily with the way he was strapped down. So, I grabbed the entire stretcher and tipped him over so the puke would not block his airways. To be sure of this, I started pulling the puke out of his mouth with my fingers. He would gasp for air and then kind of lunge. It was a good sign because it meant that he was really trying to gasp for air. Clearing his airway was a constant battle the whole time.

We still had a long flight. He had already vomited once, and I knew it would happen again. As soon as he vomited, I'd clear out his airway, roll him back over, get him a little more responsive, and then start a neuro assessment. His pupils were completely different sizes than each other. One was blown, and that's usually a sign of intracranial pressure.

We got a hold of the team at the hospital in Germany. They were prepped and waiting for us. The whole time, I was laser-focused, managing Jordan's airway and maintaining control of the hemorrhage. It was a constant fight between me and him to keep the gauze in his damn head with his life hanging in the balance. The crew chief gave me the two-minute call-out. We landed. The ramp dropped, and I saw the whole team of medics standing by, ready to take action.

We loaded him up onto the hospital's stretcher. I stayed with him, keeping my hand on his head as we rolled towards the hospital. We got to the building, the door opened, and the surgical team stood there waiting. I was so happy to see the SRT guys and all the surgeons. We got Jordan onto the table. We cut him out of the kit and got him off the stretcher. All together, we did a "one, two, three" and plumped him onto the hospital bed.

At this point, I blocked out the world and was directly in tunnel vision with Jordan and me. My adrenaline was rushing. I had my fingers in Jordan's skull long enough that I didn't want to move. All the doctors and surgeons had to tell me it was okay to let go of the wound. I remember them saying, "It's time to let go." Once I let go, the surgeons swarmed around him, around the table, and his bed. I walked behind the surgical team, listening and absorbing everything that was said. They called for blood. I was familiar with the facility. I went with someone else on the team, and we ran and grabbed units of blood and brought it over. They plugged them in. They hooked them up. And it was hands-off at that point. I stepped back and took a breath.

I don't remember who it was that came and grabbed me. I remember a lot of people coming to check on me. Everyone was traumatized by the event. But I was still in an adrenaline rush mode. But they brought me back to reality. My gear was covered in blood and brain matter. They took it off, hosed it down the best they could, and just set it aside. They gave me a bunch of water, and as I drank, I heard the helicopter take off. There were more casualties. The sound of the helicopter was my reminder that I wasn't done for the night. I had to head back out. I took a giant breath of relief. I was glad we were able to get Jordan to the hospital because it gave him the best chance to survive. I grabbed my gear, and the next thing I knew, I was on a helicopter going back out because my priority was to the task forces. My night was just beginning.

PART TWO
SAND SAILOR

IN THE BEGINNING

I love my youth. I had a blast as a kid. I grew up on Park Trail Drive in Elk Grove, California. Seven of us young boys were all within a year of each other on that block. Some of my fondest memories were created with some of the best friends a kid could ask for. It was Josh, Todd, Kirk, me, Derek, Corey, and Kevin. And of the seven of us, Kevin and I were the ringleaders of the bunch. We were the ones starting most of the trouble and leading our friends to do the dumb things that we wanted to do. The little suburb I grew up in was quiet (at least, it was when I was growing up).

Keeping ourselves entertained, we'd play silly games, reenacting our favorite movies like Tremors and Predator, and as our own gang of rag-tag boys were our own real-life version of the film *The Sandlot*. But, instead of baseball, the game we'd play the most was WAR. The game was based on the honorary system; as much as a group of six seven-year-old kids could play an honorary system. If you got shot and somebody said they hit you, it was on the person to admit they were killed. Otherwise, we'd get into arguments. I always carried Nerf guns without any bullets. We would pretend to shoot like super special forces guys running all around our neighborhood. It was an unspoken agreement between the kids, neighborhood families, and adults.

We all had a free range of backyards and fences of everyone on our street, so it wouldn't be an odd sight for one of our neighbors to see one of us carrying a toy gun sprinting across their backyard to try and get away and or trying to find a hiding spot. We were known as "those kids" in the neighborhood. Looking back, we had free reign of the whole neighborhood, and nobody stopped us. Nobody said anything to my parents, at least not that we knew of. And we would play and play and play. And there were no fundamental rules to the game either because if you got killed or shot, you just kept playing anyway. "I killed you," and then you'd just run off and try to kill somebody else. There was no winner or loser. There is no start or natural finish to the game, either. It was just a game where we chased each other around, pretending to track each other down and shoot each other without any real end goal or mission. There was no real way to win. Sometimes, we would try and spy on the older girl from across the street from my house. We would hang out and hide in a tree and watch her like weird little kids do. Looking back at those moments, playing WAR influenced me, foreshadowing what was to come.

One day, we were playing WAR, and I was running away from Kevin because he was chasing me. To lose him, I decided to jump the fence into Derek's yard into my family's yard. He lived right behind me. I remember jumping off a planter to try and grab the top of the fence. I had planned to jump, all in one move, plant my foot onto the fence, and swing over the top. Just as my foot hit the center of the fence, it snapped, and the entire board broke. I went flying back, swung my arm back hard to try and catch myself, and my forearm hit that same planter I just jumped from and broke my arm in half.

There I was, hanging off the side of the planter. My friends were terrified. It was the most horrific thing we've ever seen in our lives. They ran to get my parents. Fortunately, my mom, a nurse, knew how to stabilize my arm. She got me into the car and rushed me to the emergency room. This led to me getting a cast, which was the coolest thing ever in my mind at that point in life, like a WAR trophy, a tremendous badge of honor. What was once traumatic became the badge of honor all my friends wanted to sign and draw on.

My mom was furious, and I played WAR the rest of the day, even with my cast on. And then the next day, we'd wake up, probably do the same thing, and play WAR

again. We got our guns and started playing WAR. I was
jumping over that fence in the same direction and
manner. A cast on my arm didn't stop me. It was onto the
next game.

HIGH SCHOOL

I remember exactly where I was on September 11, 2001. I
was in high school. I was a freshman sitting at my desk in
English class when my teacher turned on the TV. I saw
everything that had happened. I don't think I realized the
gravity of that moment and how it would change everything for me, including the direction I would take with my
life and how my choice to join the military would affect
me as an adult. That moment in time had a tremendous
impact on me. A few years later, as a junior in high school,
I did a project with a group of friends. Our teacher gave
the assignment to report on the United States Special
Forces and their capabilities. I became obsessed. I idolized
the men who volunteered to fight and those willing to
sacrifice themselves for others. I wanted to be like them
and felt I could make that sacrifice, too. I knew deep down
I could do that job. I looked up to them and held all the
men and women who volunteered to fight for our country
in high regard.

When it came to joining the military, I remember not being afraid. I didn't feel nervous because I felt like this was what I was supposed to do. Weirdly, I felt comfortable and reassured that this was the path I was to take in life. From a very young age, I enjoyed physical challenges, from playing competitive soccer to wrestling to playing football to playing WAR. Joining the military was going to be the ultimate physical challenge. And everyone I knew agreed and reminded me that going into Special Forces would be the most challenging training in the world. My friends said, "If you can finish this training, then you'll be one of the baddest dudes on the planet and have accomplished something that few men ever get to do in their lives."

LIFE OPTIONS

Sometimes people ask me, "What would I have done instead if I hadn't joined the military?"

As a kid, I vividly remember watching the show "Cops" with my mom. We would talk about how good of a police officer we thought I would've been. Had I not joined the military, I probably would've gone into some first responder field, like working as a fire-fighter or police officer. But, when 9/11 happened, I became obsessed with thoughts about joining the military and what I could do in that field to serve my country. I've always been very protective by nature, especially with my friends and family. But really, I'm protective of just about anyone. It's just something that's part of my personality.

I remember, in sixth grade at Elk Grove Elementary, a young kid was getting bullied by a boy named Eric. One day, I decided that I'd take it up with Eric. School was out, and we were by the bike racks, unlocking our bikes and getting ready to go home, when I overheard Eric picking on this kid again. Oh man, it made me angry. Without another thought, I dropped my bike and defended the kid. Instinctively, I ended up getting into a fight with Eric. And it's kind of funny to think about. We didn't even really throw fists or punches. Instead, I grabbed him by the shirt and headbutted him in the nose. I told him that I didn't want to see him picking on that kid again. I was proud of myself. I didn't care if I got in trouble because I thought I was doing the right thing. But maybe breaking his nose made me the bully?

TRACK SCHOLARSHIP

During my senior year of high school, I enlisted in the Navy. I anticipated going off to boot camp and becoming a Navy SEAL shortly after graduation. I was determined. I wanted to be one of the guys who wore the American flag on their sleeve. I wanted to be someone I had looked up to all my life, the ones who fought to defend and serve our country.

It wasn't a shock to anybody that I decided to pursue the military. I had everyone's support and was overly confident I could make it and do well. Day and night, I bragged about it to my family and friends. The route I was to take with my life was evident to them. They could see the ambition in my eyes from miles away, especially from the early days of being a kid and playing WAR with my friends. They knew it was what I wanted. It was almost like they expected me to join. I was built and designed for it. And it's what I wanted to do for the rest of my life.

About a month before high school graduation, I received a scholarship offer to compete at Sacramento State University. When I got the call, I knew I had to take it. It was an opportunity of a lifetime, and I couldn't pass on it. The idea of competing at a national level as a D1 track and field athlete was a dream come true. So, I approached the

Navy and told them about the offer and how I wanted to pursue it. They allowed me to get out of my initial contract, and after being released from the contract, I was in college.

All I cared about was track and field and girls. Looking back now, I obviously had no place in college. When you're a successful high school athlete, teachers tend to be a little more lenient on academics than they otherwise would be. I didn't know what I was doing. I couldn't charm my way into extra credit and a passing grade anymore. I didn't really care about academics as much as I should have. I joined a fraternity, lived with a roommate, and spent time partying, drinking, chasing girls, running track, and doing all the things that weren't that important. Eventually, my grades slipped, and I lost my scholarship and got kicked out of school.

For a while, I felt completely lost. I no longer had any direction. I tried junior college for a few years while I still had eligibility to compete in track and field. I looked into going straight to the police academy. That was the goal for a while until I reconnected with my high school sweetheart, who was living in Southern California. I realized if I were to reenter into a contract with the Navy and still pursue my Navy SEAL aspirations, I would be stationed near her. At the time, it seemed like a great idea; I'd be able to maintain my relationship and still follow my childhood dreams of becoming a Navy SEAL.

So, I went and did what I had originally planned and set out to do: to become a Navy SEAL. I re-enlisted. Only this time, I was guaranteed a $40,000 signing bonus once I finished my training. Of course, shortly after I had enlisted back into the Navy, my high school sweetheart and I broke up again. Regardless, I was set to head to Navy Bootcamp on June 29th, 2006, where I would serve for a total of 6 years, 7 months, and 28 days.

All of which I nearly ruined when I was arrested for evading arrest. My roommates, friends, and I were all track and field kids. After a night of going out and drinking, as a send-off for me, we decided to break into Sacramento City College Stadium to run a beer mile against another frat house. A beer mile consists of running four laps around a track, chugging a beer at each lap.

After finishing, I passed out in the middle of the football field in the center of the track. And while I was out of it, the police arrived and removed all the guys I was there with. Somehow, I went unseen. I had no idea what was happening. I stumbled to get up and started walking towards the exit to find my friends, and that's when an officer's flashlight hit my face, and I heard, "Don't move!"

Somehow, in my drunken state, I made it over a barbed wire fence and into a parking lot. I guess my thought was that I needed to hide, so when I saw a few cars in the lot, I hid myself under one of them. The officer approached me, instructed me to show my hands, and told me to come out from under the car. I thought, "There's no way he's going to be able to catch me!" I rolled out, hopped to my feet, and made it about three steps before the prongs of a stun gun hit my back. And that night, I spent a few hours in jail before being released. During my court appearance a week later, all charges were dropped, and my departure date for the Navy was quickly approaching.

Regardless of how I got to boot camp and the trials I would face during my time there, joining the military would become the greatest decision of my life. The lessons I soon learned would become the foundation for who I am today.

NAVY BOOTCAMP

On day one, I felt like a big hot shot. I was in great shape. I had just finished my first season in college as a D1 track and field athlete. In my mind, I had made it. I was high on the mountain top. I was untouchable. I felt I would easily walk through the boot camp process. I couldn't have been more wrong. I started getting sharp pains in my stomach to the point that I couldn't walk. I was having a hard time standing up and moving around. I felt dizzy like I was going to pass out. Embarrassing as it was, I had to tell one of the instructors that I was having a problem.

They checked my heart rate and sent me immediately to the emergency room. I had developed appendicitis. I'm not a doctor and don't know what causes appendicitis, but trust me, it wasn't good. I wondered, "Was it stress?" It was strange because I didn't feel an ounce of stress. I thought I was all good. I couldn't believe I was spending the night in the hospital on my first day of boot camp. I couldn't join the rest of the crew or boot camp for four days! I had to be monitored to ensure my appendix didn't burst. I was quickly reminded that even being a top athlete and in the best physical condition wasn't near the physical and mental challenge I would face. I was humbled, and I knew I was up for one of the greatest challenges of my life.

To become an EOD technician, I started my journey with my first day of boot camp, a path of one step forward and two steps back. The first step was boot camp, which then led me to San Diego for SEAL training. Eventually, I moved on to BUDS, which is basic underwater demolition SEAL training. Honestly, I thought I was doing great.

I recovered from that first day of boot camp and made it to San Diego for SEAL training.

One Friday night, my girlfriend drove down from Sacramento to stay with me in Coronado for the weekend. We walked to a pizza place, had dinner, and had a great time, and then, while going back to our hotel room, I started to feel sick to my stomach. It was exactly how I felt when I first got to boot camp and struggled with appendicitis. But this time, it felt much, much worse. I was spinning around in circles. Dizzy. I couldn't speak well. I couldn't get up or move. I had my girlfriend call an ambulance. Before I knew it, I was in the hospital, yet again, in downtown San Diego at the Balboa Medical Center Naval Hospital.

I remember lying on the gurney, feeling like I was dying. I grabbed one of the nurses and yelled, "I need help!" My abdomen felt like it was going to burst. It was such excruciating pain, and I thought the nurses could help me alleviate whatever I was experiencing. The doctor joined me in the room, ran their tests, and found out that the appendicitis I had when I first joined boot camp had returned, but only this time, my appendix had burst. Not only was I in an extreme amount of pain, but my life was also in danger.

I was rushed into surgery to have my appendix removed. Meanwhile, the team I was training with in BUDS had no idea what had happened to me. I was terrified. This is what I had built my whole life up to was making it to BUDS. I had finally made it through the first two weeks, the first phase of training, and I thought I was doing really solid for myself. But now, I thought, "Oh man, I hope they don't drop me. I hope I don't get kicked out."

They reassured me that I would be okay and that they would roll me right back into where I left off. It turned out that I had to start over again, completing the entire first phase. I still can't believe my appendix burst. And my poor girlfriend, we didn't see each other after that, unfortunately.

Once I healed from my appendix removal, I was back at it again, starting round two of BUDS class. At this point, I thought, "What's the worst that can happen to me other than my appendix bursting?" I know it was a cocky thought at the time, but it helped push me to keep going. I thought I knew what was going to come in the upcoming weeks. I knew how miserable it would be, and my buddies had already told me some of the secrets, so I thought I had an edge.

I was about to go through one of the hardest trainings in the world. I thought, "If I can just make it to Hell Week, I'll be one step closer than I was the last time I tried, and this time I could make it through the rest of it." That was my mindset.

We were up at four o'clock and out in the open ocean every day. I was swimming with my buddy, Sam. We made time, no problem. And as soon we were out of the water, we were back in our uniforms, running miles on the beach. We ran non-stop and being one of the guys in better shape and running form, I was always near the front of the pack. However, this day, I was at the back of the pack and was one of the last guys in line. I couldn't catch my breath. I felt like I couldn't open my lungs enough to let air into my chest. I kept running. I was struggling. It was like I was breathing through a snorkel or a hose. I knew it wasn't a problem with my appendix. My stomach didn't hurt. This time, it was my chest.

I just couldn't take a big enough breath to keep running, and eventually, I started to panic. And then, before I knew it, I was passed out on the beach. I woke up with an instructor in my face. Sure enough, I had blacked out during the run, and they found me lying in the sand. They called a medic, who checked me out and cleared my airways. Turns out, I had what was called swim-induced pulmonary edema (SIPE), caused by getting too much water into the lungs from underwater and surface swimming. I couldn't believe it! I had developed full-blown pneumonia from breathing in water while I was swimming. Here I was, in the middle of my second attempt at BUDS training, recovering from another injury. The thought of starting again and going into my third attempt was beyond frustrating. I imagined the team, my buddies from my class, whom I started this whole training with, graduating by the time I was beginning my third attempt. Such bullshit! I couldn't catch a break. I was breaking down mentally, and it was apparent that my body couldn't keep up.

By the third attempt, I was not as mentally confident as I had been the two prior times. I thought, "What's going to break now?" Mentally, I felt like I still had some in me. I knew I could do it, but I was just worried that my body wouldn't be able to keep up with me. Thankfully, this time around, I received one of the highest marks in the obstacle courses. And oddly enough, I was one of the lead swimmers in my class. I performed at a higher level and got paired with the slower swimmers. They made it my job to guide them, pull them through the swim, and help them get qualifying times. I think my instructors were hoping that my leadership and skillset could improve. In any case, I made it through and was off to Hell Week.

Hell Week was just as terrible as it sounds. The guns would go off, and bam, Hell Week started. At first, it's shocking. Flashbangs, smoke grenades, guns with blanks are firing, and it's just chaos. We're running around working out while getting screamed at and sprayed with a fire hose. And I'm reveling in it. All I thought was, "This is what I've been waiting for!" I was finally in it. I was doing it. I knew that if I got through it, I would make the rest of it, or at least that's what I hoped. I thought, "If I can make it through this, then I can make it through anything."

They had us running with boats on our heads, carrying logs out of all things. I remember doing what felt like miles upon miles of lunges on the beach with these huge, heavy logs on my head. At least I was there with the other guys. There were five of us in each boat crew. Our arms were burning. And some of us were tearing up. You could see the worry in each other's eyes. We were all wondering if we could make it and get a score, but we were starting to break.

We hit the surf, wet and sandy, and then we lined up. We were allowed a short break while standing beside our boats at the bottom of the berm. And then it was time to run. Once again, I was one of the better athletes. I thought, "Come on, Jordan. I know you can do this." Running is not a problem for me. I wanted to be one of the first guys. I needed to catch a break and get the advantage of being a winner. So, I'm flying. I'm running as hard as I can. I'm making sure I'm up near the front of the pack. As we make it down to the gates of the North Island on Coronado Beach, I stop to turn around and see that I'm the third guy in my class who has touched the fence. I turn to start running back, and I feel extremely confident. I'm happy. But then, my right knee started to hurt. It began to buckle with every step I took, pounding into the ground. I remember thinking, "Oh no, here it goes again." Something for sure was happening. My body was breaking. I tried to block it out and keep running. I'm thinking, "It's just shin splints. I can run through that." A lot of guys get shin splints. I'll make it.

I end up racing past everyone. My instructor, Del Los Reyes, instructed me to tell the guys (who finished after me) to hit the surf. Hitting the surf is when you go out in the ocean and do flutter kicks. The guys came running towards me one by one. I followed orders. And thought, "I hope my instructor remembers that I was in front of the pack so I can catch a break." But instead, Reyes came towards me and started yelling in my face, "Get down and do pushups!" I did so many that I can't even remember the count. Then he told me to hit the surf with the rest of my crew. And that was the moment I broke.

I was devastated. I put everything I could into that run. I was a winner. I deserved that break. I guess winning was never the point. The point was to get broken mentally. And they won. They got me there. They called us out of the water. "Come line up with your crew next to your boat." I hobbled. My knee was busted. Shivering and sore, we all lined up in our boat crews to reassign crews as guys were quitting.

And this is where I feel the most embarrassed, to tell the truth about what happened. I was so mentally broken that they got me. They accomplished their goal, and that was to find someone that would break. I broke. My boat crew kept saying, "No, Jordan! Stay." But I had to do what I had to do. I couldn't do it anymore. From having my appendix burst to getting pneumonia to now a busted knee. I walked up, and I quit.

To this day, it's hard for me to say it out loud. I quit BUDS. I never saw myself as a quitter. Now, I was faced with a choice of what to do next. Since I was still under a specialized contract, I would have to find something else to do. I first decided to interview with the Navy Dive

School. And then one of the instructors I had befriended at BUDS said, "Why don't you look into EOD technician training."

I watched this video of what an EOD was. An EOD's mission was more focused on the safety of our men. This would be my redemption, a second chance to fulfill my childhood dreams. Specializing in explosives and disarming bombs was right up my alley. It sounded like my kind of fun.

I interviewed with the EOD Master Chief, and I remember him telling me, "Well, you quit BUDS. Why would we waste our time sending you to EOD school if you're just going to quit?" That caught me off guard. I didn't have an answer. He was right. I had built up this façade and dream of becoming a Navy SEAL and had just quit because I couldn't do it. How would I convince him that I wouldn't quit EOD school? I tried to look devastated. I gave him a laundry list of excuses, "Well, I had pneumonia, my appendix was removed, and my body was just falling apart, and my knee was still bothering me a little bit." I didn't really emphasize telling him about my knee because I wanted him to recruit me. I emphasized the fact that I didn't quit. "I didn't quit after my appendix burst. I didn't quit after getting pneumonia. And I for damn sure wasn't going to quit again." I thought, "If given the opportunity, I would show him I could do it again. I'd make it."

EOD SCHOOL

For whatever reason, he decided to take a chance on me. I was on my way to EOD school. Coming from my background with academics and not doing so hot, I knew I had to bring it. EOD school is one of the most academically challenging schools in the military. They have you take tests every single week in all different subjects. And if you fail, you get one chance to make it up. Fail two tests? You're done. It's very high stress. Typically, those who get into EOD have already been in the military and served.

The EOD school pipeline starts at the Panama City Beach, Florida, Navy dive school. Dive school was a requirement for Navy EOD as we dealt with underwater bombs as well. EOD dive school is typically the hardest part of the EOD training pipeline. Our instructor yelled verbal commands during one PT (physical training) session. Starting EOD school, I felt revitalized and back to my confident, cocky self. This was evident when I yelled back, "Don't threaten us with a good time!" My response instigated a slew of insults and upped the intensity of our instructors for that PT! Luckily, my class was in good

enough spirits. We all laughed and suffered the consequences happily. "Don't threaten us with a good time"
even became a motto for our class after that.

After leaving Navy Dive school, I returned to my hometown of Elk Grove, California, to marry Krista. Krista
helped nurse me back to health, and we stayed together
through all the ups and downs of BUDS into EOD
school. We had a short window to get to the courthouse,
get married, and drive back to Fort Walton Beach, Florida.
The class didn't wait for me while I was on leave getting
married; they were off, and I had to start the next phase of
EOD school without them and wait for the next Navy
class to start.

I met with my new class and seamlessly rolled in with
these guys as though I had been with them from the start.
I was grateful this was a class I fit in well with. The
following 42 weeks were gonna be hard! In those 42
weeks, we would cover 9 different subjects, from basic
demolition to growing in difficulty at each new phase. We
had to become experts in every field of conventional and
unconventional ordinance. I barely graduated high school,
I was a college dropout, and now I was an expert in the
science behind our most dangerous nuclear weapons.

I was trained at the Air Force base in Florida. Before getting to EOD school, I had to pass Navy Dive School, where I learned how to mix gas and dive deep water scuba. We had to learn how to get off ships and disarm underwater bombs and mines that rest at the bottom of the sea. I had to pass all that before I ever learned how to disarm bombs dropped from planes and learn about improvised explosive devices (IEDs), which is everything that we saw in Iraq and Afghanistan. Our lives depended upon our proficiency, which was vital to becoming extremely proficient and skilled to survive.

Disarming bombs is like playing chess. You have to have a creative mindset. You can make multiple moves to achieve whatever goal you're trying to accomplish. It doesn't matter; whatever bomb you're disarming, there are always multiple angles and directions that you can take to disarm them. I pride myself on having the ability to solve puzzles. I tackle challenges from all angles. That's basically what disarming bombs is all about. It's a cat-and-mouse game; the bomb builder doesn't want me to solve his puzzle, so the EOD tech has to assess all possibilities.

PARACHUTE MALFUNCTIONS

A perk of being in the special forces is that I got to go to different schools. And when we weren't actively deployed, we were training. Free fall school. Skydiving. I was already airborne qualified and static line qualified to jump out of planes, even with 367 skydives under my belt. I had to further my training. I had to learn to jump out of a parachute at 30,000 feet under oxygen. Being the adrenaline junkie that I am, it was exhilarating. I had only ever done solo skydives. I had never done a single tandem skydive from start to finish. Usually, we'd go with an instructor, and they'd fly with us. They would help us and teach us how to fly correctly so we wouldn't make any mistakes. But otherwise, I was always solo, and once under the canopy, you're on your own figuring out how to land.

Statistically, one in every 500 jumps is when something malfunctions. In that case, you have to cutaway to get your main canopy to open. I had always handled myself well under pressure. But the first time my parachute malfunctioned was one of the single scariest moments of my life.

I was in free fall. I hit my 10,000 mark and then 5,000, and that's when I pulled my parachute. It opened, but only partially. The chute's opening slowed me down enough to look up. I tried to pull down on my steering toggles. One of them was tied in a knot, which made the knot tighter as I pulled. I lost control. Trying to steer my canopy, I couldn't get a grip, and I was spinning, turning, and descending through the air column. I thought, "This could be it." If I couldn't cut away from my main canopy, my reserve canopy wouldn't open, and I'd burn into the ground. I thought I'd probably break some bones and definitely get hurt. I had enough time to think about the consequences. I chose to cut away my main canopy and deploy my reserves. I put both hands on each handle to pull. I was thousands of feet above the ground. I didn't have a choice. I pulled both cords, and the spin of the canopy threw me in the air like a slingshot.

The acceleration was unlike anything I'd ever experienced before. My stomach turned. I watched my main canopy spin and flutter to the ground. Adrenaline pumped through my body. I felt almost unable to breathe. I was overwhelmed with excitement and fear. I remember landing on the ground. The mental challenge I had to face during that moment was something I'd never forget. I had a few other malfunctions during the 300 and some jumps I took after that, but nothing quite like the first. The more it happened, the more confident I became, knowing I could handle it if something terrible happened.

SURVIVAL SCHOOL

I was required to attend SERE School. SERE stands for survival, evasion, resistance, and escape. It's where we military guys learn how to defend ourselves and survive if we ever become POWs (prisoners of war). It's where we learn how to operate within the Geneva Convention Rules. And it's where we learn what we're allowed to say if we were ever to be captured.

The training is intense. The first week, you learn how to pick locks and handcuffs. You learn different survival tools, ensuring you use a compass correctly and hitting certain marks and targets through the mountains. And then you spend a week in the woods where you have to survive for a week. At the end of that week, you spend a few days with your instructors, who become your enemy. They hunt you. They capture you. Ultimately, every single person ends up getting captured. And then, you learn what living as a POW is like. SERE's school was extremely difficult for me to finish.

They challenged us to use our environment and the materials around us to build something. I used sticks, vines, and branches to make a chair. I used the chair as my walker, and it also came in handy when I had to go to the bathroom. I earned an orange for winning that challenge.

That was the first thing I had eaten that week. They fed us rabbit after they showed us how to kill and skin it. I sucked the eyeball out of the rabbit. It felt like a grape but tasted like a bitter, metallic type of metal.

Being held captive, they instructed us not to give anybody any information, even if we were being tortured or interrogated. I took the assignment very literally. I don't know if my buddies could say the same. They asked for my mom's name. I kept saying, "I call her mom, Sir. Her name is Mom." I didn't budge. Again, they'd yell, "What's your mother's name?" And I'd continue to say, "I call her mom." After the third or fourth time, I got smacked. They were allowed to hit us if it was an open palm.

This guy's hands were humongous. When he hit me on the left side of my cheek, my right side felt it, too. His hand wrapped around my face. He asked again, "What's your mom's name?" He wouldn't get off that question. I dug my heels in and thought, "There's no way they'll get me to budge. I'm not gonna break." I knew it was a challenge of my will versus theirs, and I was determined to win. I wasn't going to let them break me.

So, I continued with the same answer. "Her name is mom, Sir. I call her mom. My mom's name is mom." And then he hit me again. This one stung. It rang out in my mind for hours. They finally released us to go back into our prison cells, where we had little blocks of wood to use as pillows or chairs. They'd play music and the sounds of crying babies all night long. I think they ultimately wanted us to try and escape out of prison, but none of us ever accomplished it. We just got beat up until it was time to go home. When SERE's school was finally over, I was driving home and looked in my rear-view mirror for the first time. I saw that I had two black eyes. Those open palm slaps that I had received left me with bruises.

I look back at that experience and talk to people who are instructors at SERE's school to realize the torture situations we were in were only for a few minutes. What true POWs experience are moments that feel more like eternity. I feel for them. School is obviously different from a real-life situation. And I was fortunate to go home afterward. The first thing I ate was sushi at one of my favorite places ever, Sushi Diner in San Diego. And then I went home, took a shower, and cried. It was the single most challenging training, not only physically but mentally, that I had ever been through.

TRAINING 24/7

After completing EOD school, I had the opportunity to pick which unit I wanted to join. I originally picked NAS Sigonella Sicily, Italy. The opportunity to live in another country sounded like a great adventure! To my young wife, it was too far away from family. With my marriage struggling, I went to my chain of command and requested to be reassigned to a unit in San Diego so I could try to salvage my marriage. At that time, there weren't any spots at any of the San Diego-based Units. Luckily, a last-minute opening with the EOD mobile unit one (EOD-MU1) sealed my fate. I was sent to San Diego. I was super motivated to be out of training and do my job.

On arrival, the EODMU1 had no teams to assign me to. This was why there were originally no openings, but my marriage was getting put back together. A few weeks later, I got a phone call while I was at work: we were going to have a baby! But without a team, they had me working administratively in the head office. As the bottom of the totem pole guy, they had me doing paperwork, janitorial duties, and things like taking out the trash and vacuuming. It was boring, to say the least, but I guess I was earning my stripes.

As a 22-year-old, in true Jordan fashion, I would get in trouble regularly for not shaving and being a few minutes late every so often. Without a team yet to join, I lacked purpose and motivation. I would push the limits with my leadership to see what parts of my personality I could show off and get away with. And that's not something to be praised or looked at as good. Because in the military, you need to be part of a team, not an individual, goofing around doing things your own way, which was a lesson I learned over time.

I was finally placed on a team that would deploy, a deployment I wouldn't make. A team where, for some reason, my chief and I just never got along. Naturally, I pushed against it to the point where I got in trouble and found myself paying a visit to the captain's mast, which is military lingo to say you screwed up for punishment but not bad enough for charges, a non-judicial punishment. It is not a good place to be. One can lose rank, resulting in a loss of pay and removal from his team. Regardless of my relationship with my chief, this captain's mast was my fault.

I got captain's mast. I had to get in my dress uniform and present my case to the officer in charge of EODMU1. My crime- I had borrowed one of my teammate's belts for the uniform of that day with his permission. On another day, I had forgotten my belt again at home. Without thought, I went and took my teammate's belt to use it again, and that's when I was reported to have stolen his gear. Word got up to the chain of command that I stole something. I didn't even think this was stealing because it was right back where it was initially at the end of the day. I realize now the whole thing was a misunderstanding, but either way, I was wrong. It was my fault.

Because of that captain's mast and my disagreement and butting heads with the leadership on that team, I ended up at very shallow water (VSW), which was part of the mine warfare program, also known as the black sheep of EODMU1. I fit right in with the bunch of Marine Recon guys, a Navy diver, and a dive medic. We were responsible for diving in very shallow water to clear any minefields that could impact possible boat lanes. Fortunately for me, I loved this job. We were all good at it. I loved working with the Recon Marines; ultimately, they became some of the best friends I could ever have. It was the perfect routine in the gym, lifting as heavy as possible and jacked up on pre-workout supplements. Then, into the water for the rest of the day. The guys on that team are some of the only ones I have kept in touch with outside the military to this day. We were efficient at using the Viper, a rebreather type of rig that uses a fully closed-circuit gas mixture with bubbleless operation. The Viper was low profile low magnetic signature. Ideal for covert operations. We could locate and ultimately destroy underwater mines using an EOD-specific handheld sonar, ensuring safe passage by our naval vessels.

During VSW, we were constantly training. We were always practicing and maintaining our gear. We did rehearsals, practicing our jobs so that if we were ever called to duty, we could execute our jobs perfectly. This is the case for a lot of military type of jobs that aren't routinely deployable. It's just practicing and rehearsing every day for the off chance of an emergency. It is better to have us and not need us than need us and not have us.

The guys and I knew how to make training fun. Since we spent most of our time in the waters of the San Diego Bay, we would dive for lobster. We didn't do it all the time, but it made for good eating on the days that we did. We'd come in with ten to twenty lobster tails and have a barbecue back in the shop. It was a blast. That time with the VSW team was technically short, non-deployable duty. It could have been deployable duty, but the current conflict was in a desert. Fortunately, we were never used to that function. Later, I was assigned to a team that would deploy to Afghanistan with a team of Army Rangers. I would utilize all the EOD training I had acquired over the years. As the EOD guys, we would most likely be running point for these teams, ensuring the safest routes to and from operations.

I wish I had more of a picturesque story to explain my time in San Diego before my deployment with the Rangers and what would be my first and final deployment. Honestly, the military was not a glamorous experience. When people see me and hear that I was in the military, I get asked how many tours I had. To their surprise," only one" isn't what they expect. They think I must have jaw-dropping stories to tell. But that wasn't my story. Like I said, I spent a lot of time practicing, learning, and training. And most of it was spent in the safe environment of San Diego, which made for easy days.

Being in the military was like playing on an athletic team. You have your season when you're playing your sport. You're actually doing it. And then you have your off-season, where you're preparing for the next season. When deployed, you're in season and utilizing all the skills and techniques, or "plays," that we learned during the off-season. Off-season is when we're home, improving our skills, learning, and going to different types of schools to get schooled. Now that I was moving from VSW to deploy with the Rangers, I got my call off the bench to the big leagues.

DEPLOYMENT

It was an incredible feeling to be suited up in my uniform with boots on the ground in Afghanistan with my team. You could ask a hundred different people who've been deployed, and you'll get a hundred different answers. But for me, it was something I had really looked forward to. I wasn't scared, I was excited. I grew up wanting to do it. I was chasing my dream of serving my country as a warfighter. It was something I reveled in and was very proud of. I could've benefited from a little bit of fear. It might have kept me safer, but I was kind of always the crazy kid who was brave and willing to try anything. As that old saying goes, would you jump off a cliff if your best friend did?

I am the kid who jumped first; that's just who I am and who I'll always be. I loved getting the opportunity to go overseas and do my job with a group of guys who trusted one another to keep each other safe, literally our lives in each other's hands, something that I'm still so proud of to this day. It's a bonding experience like no other. Plus, it was everything I had always been waiting to do, and what I had been training for years for. I was finally getting the opportunity to fulfill the job requirements for what I signed up for. My job was dangerous, and most people avoid doing it. I was very proud to finally begin the experience of doing it for real. I felt it in my body. This is where I was supposed to be. I loved it. It was my identity. It's who I was, who I wanted to be. It was everything to me. I saw my deployment as an honored privilege and looked forward to it.

The first thing that hit me the second I arrived was how cold it was. Everyone always assumes that Afghanistan is always this hot, messy desert. And I'm sure at some points it is extremely hot and uncomfortable. But, since I was there in December, it was freezing cold. A ton of snow was on the ground, and it was just painfully cold. Shivering profusely, we all huddled together, trying to find any warmth we could while on the tarmac, waiting for helicopters. The type of cold that would take your breath away.

A perk of being deployed with Army Rangers is we had our own little section of the base where we had our own rooms, even our own gym. The room I was assigned to was designed for two people. It was a bunk bed type of thing, but I was the only one in there. I thought it was strange because, from what everyone's told me, that's uncommon and not what typically happens. They kept calling me Sergeant, which led me to believe there was a little mix-up because the Army doesn't understand the Navy's ranking system, and vice versa. The military's ranking systems are different, so I think they stuck me in the room for a Sergeant, which was two ranks above me. I liked the room, so I went with it, and they all called me Sergeant the whole time. I brought a TV from the States on deployment and set up my Xbox. During downtime, I'd play Xbox games and talk to my wife using the base computers. My deployment was only eight days, but the routine for every day I was there was the same. Wake up, work out, prep gear, and attend intel meetings for that night's operation. Go out, execute the operation, come home, try to get as much sleep as possible, and then do that same cycle over again. Of the eight days I was deployed in Afghanistan, I operated every night I was there. It was a very high workload, which was just a part of doing special operations. That eighth day started just the same as all the others, but by the end of that day, I would be forever changed, and my life would be completely different from that point on.

PART THREE
GROUND ZERO

UNIFORMED MEN AT THE DOOR

Krista Stevenson

December 16, 2011, was the last time I talked to Jordan before he was shot. I was at the Naval Medical Center in San Diego for a dermatology appointment, a place known for lack of cell phone service, when I received a call from Jordan from a satellite phone. He called to say hi and to let me know he was headed out on a mission. Our son, Kayden, was two years old and home with my dad. My dad came down to pack up our house and put things into storage while Jordan was deployed. I planned to head north with Kayden to spend time with family and save money while we waited for Jordan to come home. Jordan and I discussed the whole plan and decided it was best not to pack before his deployment. We didn't want to spend our last days together that way.

After a long day of packing that evening, I took a break. I pulled out my laptop, nestled into our large beige sectional, and flipped on the television that was mounted on the wall in front of me. I pulled up our e-mail account while Kayden played and entertained himself with his toys. I became used to hearing from Jordan. He would call or send an e-mail, usually between the hours of six and eight at night. I hadn't heard from him. We shared an e-mail account to e-mail internally back and forth. It was easy this way. We enjoyed being able to see if our messages had been opened or not.

That night, when I logged into our account, I was sad and a little surprised that he hadn't opened the message I sent him the night before. I was feeling bummed about Christmas and struggling to get into the spirit without him. It was weird because it was the first year he wouldn't be around for the holidays. Looking at the unopened message in the inbox, I thought it was unusual. He always wrote me back. I brushed it off, assuring myself that his mission probably went longer than expected. Nothing to panic about. I was sure I would hear from him in the next day or two.

The following day, I heard my dad working in my bedroom, breaking down and bubble wrapping some of the larger furniture items in our bedroom, when I was caught off guard by a knock at the front door. Jordan and I lived in a small two-bedroom, one-bathroom house just a few blocks from the beach with a small front yard fully fenced in with a large gate that we kept shut most of the time. With Rylie, our four-year-old Rottweiler/Doberman mix, constantly in and out of the house, it was rare that we would get an unexpected knock at the door.

Instead of my eyes being met with the abundance of purple morning lilies that lined our fence, I saw three men in full navel dress uniforms standing at attention as my mind went blank for a split second, searching for a feeling of existence. My thoughts raced. I tried to figure out why they were there. I was frozen. "May we come in?" I reached forward to open the screen door to let them in. I was overwhelmed by internal sickness, burdened with questions, and unable to speak. The three uniformed men stood in perfect formation, poised cordially in my living room. Before I could speak, they suggested I should probably take a seat. My mind finally reconnected with my mouth, "Is he okay?"

Curious to the knock on the door, my dad stood in the doorway to the right of the television. They removed their hats in respect and said, "There's been an accident tonight." Without pausing, they continued to describe what happened to Jordan during the previous night's mission. Jordan was hurt, and it was severe. He had been shot. The bullet was believed to have penetrated the left side of his skull. It finally made sense. That's why he hadn't opened my message.

Jordan was still in Afghanistan in critical condition after being put in a medically induced coma because of the brain surgery that was performed earlier that evening.

The thought of him having brain surgery sent me into a spiral. I drifted in and out of the conversation. I was over-come with disbelief. How could this be happening? I had just talked to Jordan. I had just heard his voice. It had only been eleven days since his deployment. And now, I couldn't help but think he had left the earth entirely. Were Kayden and I left to face life alone because he was never coming home?

I broke eye contact with the uniformed men and looked at my son embraced in my dad's arms. I was stunned. I stared at Kayden. It was torturing to remember the happi-ness and excitement that would light up his face when-ever his dad arrived home from work. I wanted this nightmare to end. I had to go to bed that night knowing my husband was in a medically induced coma and wondering if and when he would ever return.

I CAN HEAR YOU

After surviving Afghanistan, I was transferred to Land-stuhl Regional Medical Center (LRMC), a military hospital in Germany. Thankfully, my family was able to fly in from the States to say their goodbyes. My mom, Michelle, sister, Amber, and wife Krista were there. I was still in a medically induced coma when they arrived, and I wasn't supposed to wake up.

Amber stood next to my bed, not knowing if this would be the last time she would see her brother. She had a medical practice back home in the States and needed to return. She held my hand and said, "If you can hear me, squeeze my hand." I squeezed back. She said, "I'm leaving. I'm sorry. I have to go. I love you. My thoughts and prayers are with you." At that moment, she knew I would be okay and would see me soon. And then, as she began to walk away, unprompted, I lifted my left hand and gave her a thumbs up. All while I was still in a coma, an unexplainable action. I think it was my way of telling her, "I can hear you, and I'll be okay." The initial care at the LRMC stabilized me enough to move me back to the States. I was still in a coma, but things were looking up.

AM I DEAD?

After I was put into a medically induced coma in Germany and stable enough to be moved, they transported me to Walter Reed Hospital in the States. I wasn't supposed to wake up, and nobody anticipated me waking up any time soon. Alone in my hospital room with a tracheotomy tube coming out of my neck, I.V. lines through my veins, heart sensors attached to my body, and a feed tube running through my nose, I lie there wide awake. I didn't know where I was or who I was with. What was happening? What happened to me? I was terrified and started to panic. Somehow, I remembered the gunfight. But then I thought, am I dead? Am I in hell? I couldn't be. Not in this dark room. This isn't heaven.

I panicked. The only thing left was to fire out questions in my mind and try my best to move. I had a neck brace and couldn't move my head. Where was I? Why was I here? I tried to sit up, but my right arm didn't move. I wanted to push myself again, but my right arm and leg didn't follow. I tried to open my eyes but couldn't see anything past my blurred vision. I couldn't speak. I didn't know what to do. There was nothing I could do except lay there and panic. I was terrified and clueless. Soon, the nurses got word and figured out I was lying awake. They came into my room to stabilize me the best they could and told me my family was on their way. I've done a lot of scary things in my life. But waking up in that hospital was hands down the most terrifying thing I have ever experienced in my life to date.

GET THE FUCK OUT OF MY ROOM!

Moments after waking up from my coma are blurry. The whole thing was traumatic, to say the least. Soon after, the nurses helped me calm down, my family showed up, and the doctor came to talk to me. I remember thinking this can't be real. He told me that I was shot in the head. I had lost the use of my right arm and leg, and because of that, I was never going to be able to walk again. I was paralyzed on the right side of my body. He said it's not going to be easy for you to talk. And then gave me the ultimate prognosis, "You're going to be disabled for the rest of your life." In that moment, I couldn't help myself. Anger came over me. I thought, "He doesn't know me. This can't be how the rest of my life is going to be. This doctor has no clue who I am, what I'm capable of, and what I've been through in my life. He doesn't know how talented and strong I am." Confused, angry, and heavily medicated, I said, "Get the fuck out of my room!"

This whole time, my family was worried and waiting for me to wake up from my coma. They kept wondering, "What's Jordan going to be like? What if he's not the same? What if his personality is gone?" Before I woke up, the doctors informed my family that I wouldn't be able to speak or have any cognitive function at all. So, when they heard me say those words to the doctor, it gave them the relief they all needed. It was proof that I was still in there, still fighting, and still going strong. My family was like, "There he is." That's the Jordan we all know.

FINDING A WAY TO COMMUNICATE

Talking wasn't easy. And I never really had a chance to talk more than the nurses allowed me to. I still had a tube in my trachea and couldn't speak. I had to find a way to communicate with my family and anyone who came into my room. Most of the time, I would nod and shake my head. Until I got my hands on an iPad. I figured out how to write, and somehow, I was writing sentences, which everyone was surprised when that happened. I wasn't supposed to do that because the area in my brain that controls language and speech was supposed to have been damaged the most. That didn't matter to me. I was determined and figured out how to carry on a conversation. I started to ask questions like, "Is my team okay? Did anyone else get hurt?" Thankfully, I was told my team was fine. I was the only one who was hurt that night on my team.

WHAT HAPPENED TO ME?

Though I don't remember the night of my wounds in trying to put the mental pieces together, my imagination filled the gaps for me. I was haunted by images of what my imagination believed happened to me. Nightmares I will carry with me for the rest of my life. Waking up in that hospital, not knowing where I was, what was going on, and having no control over my life and what was happening to me was terrifying. All the PTSD I have and carry with me today comes from waking up in Walter Reed. No amount of combat or wartime affected me because I knew where I was and what I was doing, and it was my choice to be there. I was so angry and lost. I didn't want to be disabled. I wasn't happy that I survived. I was upset that I didn't die in combat doing what I loved. Living this kind of life was never in the plans, and it sucked. I was comfortable with death but not with being disabled.

Ask any active-duty military service or first responders, and they will tell you that part of the job is being mentally prepared for the possibility of death. We know it's always something that can happen, so we're prepared for it. I know some guys who serve in the Army Rangers who are actively deployed, have prosthetic legs, and are really hardcore dudes. Some of them are my friends. And I've thought, if I ever had my leg blown off, that's something I can work through and deal with. But I was not mentally prepared to be shot in the head and go through the mental and heavy disabilities that come with a traumatic brain injury, losing the use of my right arm and leg, losing the movement of the right side of my face, and struggling with memory and words. I wasn't prepared for that. I would've been okay with death but not prepared to be disabled.

The thought of it all, being paralyzed and being told that I would never be the same again, was devastating. Athletic Jordan was all I had ever been. My whole life revolved around my physical and athletic abilities. Athletics made me popular in high school. My athleticism is what I was able to lean on to push me through all the military training. My physical strength took me to the places I wanted to go and why the military kept believing in me and letting me through all that training. I've always been physically present, so losing my athletic ability felt like I lost myself. I lost my life. It felt like that's where Jordan died. I didn't know who else to be. I didn't want to be a different Jordan. I struggled to accept this new reality. I had only valued the strong, athletic, physical me. I felt hopeless and out of control. I didn't know how to do this life. I was at rock bottom. That was the lowest point of my life.

WHAT TOOK YOU SO LONG?

My friends, Kevin Tatom and David Peterson, visited me at Walter Reed. The moment they found out, they dropped everything to come see me. I was in bad shape, to say the least, but I wanted them to be there. It was important for me to see my friends and get my support network around me. I also wanted them to give me a blessing to aid in my recovery. I wasn't that religious growing up. I went to church here and there. Kevin and David were members of the same church that I went to. After high school, I never went back, but that's changed. I do now. I asked them to pray for me. Seeing them and getting their blessing gave me motivation to strive. I thought if these guys were going to make an effort to come see me, I owed it to them to put in the work. I owed to them to try to get better. To show them that I was worth it and that I was strong enough to survive. I wanted to show them that the things they believed about me from all the years we spent growing up and them getting to know me were true. I could be unstoppable. And to do that, I needed to build myself a ladder.

A FRIENDS PERSPECTIVE

Kevin Tatom

I had just gone to sleep around 1:00 a.m. that night. I believe it was a Saturday night. Around 2:00 a.m., I got a call from Jordan's wife, Krista. "Hi Kevin, sorry it's so late, but I had to call you." She was crying heavily, and I feared the worst. "Jordan got shot in the head," she exclaimed. I shot out of bed. "What the heck happened?" She then told me they don't necessarily think he passed away, but all she knows is that Jordan was shot. I paced my living room for an hour before sitting down in my lazy boy and watching TV until the sun came up. I had never even thought about this as a possibility. J was almost indestructible growing up. We did some of the craziest stuff together, which always turned out okay. A few weeks later, Jordan's mom told me they were flying him to Bethesda, Maryland. A week later, she called me so that I could talk to him over the phone. He couldn't talk back, but I just kept thinking, he has to come out of this. This can't be how this ends.

A few days later, our friend David Peterson and I flew to Bethesda. Jordan was almost unrecognizable. The prognosis looked bleak. His trachea was infected, and the swelling in his head made him nauseous all the time.

When we spoke to the doctor, he said he won't ever walk again and probably won't be able to talk either. I was devastated. We went back to the hotel that night, and David and I spoke about the good times with Jordan. We prayed for his recovery and went to bed.

The following day, we woke up and went into the hospital. As we walk into the room, Jordan says in a crackled voice, "What the fuck took you guys so long." Apparently, in the early morning hours, his brain fixed itself enough for him to figure out he could type. He started typing to the nurses and communicating. A few hours later, he started saying small snippets of words, and by the time we walked in, he could talk. The following five or six years would be really hard. I was building a business and a family in Utah, but I always came to see Jordan every year. He made huge improvements each year, making the staff laugh while we were there and talking about what he would eventually accomplish. Jordan is basically my brother; I have known him since we were 4 and 5. I am so proud of the fight that dude has in him. The fight to never give up, to have the resolve to be successful after his accident, to not let his injuries define him negatively, to be a good father and husband. Jordan's story is the true American Dream. He fought for us and continues to show the world that a strong mindset is all you need. I am sure he often thinks about his previous athletic accomplishments as they are many and grand, but they pale in comparison to the man he has become and what he has overcome. I love you, man, and I can't wait to see what's next for you in life.

FEAR

When I was in the hospital, I was on suicide watch most of the time. I kept getting stuck thinking about all the things I couldn't do. All the what-ifs-

What if I can't get better?

What if I can't walk again?

What if I can't be a better dad?

What if I can't ever drive a car again?

All these thoughts of can't(s) drove into my head. Sometimes, I felt like I couldn't get past them. And having the doctors tell me that I wouldn't be able to do the things I used to do before made it hard to stay confident. Sometimes, it felt pointless, like there wasn't a reason to push through it all. But somewhere in my misery, I decided to keep going. I wanted to prove to everyone just how strong I was and just how strong I am. I wanted to shove it in the doctor's face- the one who told me I would never walk again, that I could do all of it. And more. All I kept thinking was, "Watch me!" Watch me do what I can do. Doubting my abilities was the fire that motivated me to keep going, to prove everyone wrong, and not only to get better but to live a fulfilling, happy life and still have meaning.

A SIGN OF HOPE

The recovery I was building for myself started with me believing that there was a chance that I could get better. It was no joke. I had to learn how to reframe my thoughts. If I wanted to get better, I had to stop thinking about all the things I was telling myself that I couldn't do. And start thinking about the things that I wanted to do. And all the things that I could do. I decided to repeat to myself two simple words, "I can," instead of letting the what-ifs turn negative.

What if I do get better?

What if I can walk again?

What if I can be a better dad?

What if I can drive a car again?

Krista was visiting me at Walter Reed. I was lying there at three o'clock in the morning. I couldn't sleep. I was trying to focus all my attention on moving my leg. I wanted it to happen bad. I had heard people talk about how important it is to focus all your attention on what you want to have happen, and it will happen. Like reaching out my hand to grab something, and by concentrating, that's how it'll begin to move.

At that moment, I decided to focus on moving my leg. And for the very first time, my right quadricep flexed! Krista and I were shocked. I was so excited. What else could I do that they told me I couldn't do? I called my mom, who was staying at the Fisher House, "I moved my leg!" I was so excited, and I had the nurses come in. I had them touch my leg, I would flex it, and sure enough, it would move! Something so little was so big for me. And from that point on, everything started to change. That little bit of momentum was all I needed to push me to do bigger and better things.

NURSE MCGIBBON

I started making progress with physical therapy. I'll never forget Nurse McGibbon. He was the epitome of care. The extra time he spent with me wasn't required. His dedication to my well-being was the support and accountability I needed. In between therapy sessions, he'd hang out with me on his breaks while eating lunch. He was always there, especially when my family wasn't around to keep me company. He believed in me and wanted to see me succeed. Day after day, he would come to my room to hang with me. He'd get me to inch over to the side of my bed where I could let my feet dangle. He would get underneath my arms to support the weight of my body. He held me upright so I could safely stand up next to my bed. I'd shift my weight back and forth to start developing patterns and muscle memory of getting weight on my legs. After doing this with me daily, I began to make progress. Eventually, our time together turned into him putting both arms around my chest, holding me upright, and helping me take baby steps around my hospital bed until one of us got tired. I'm not sure if he did this with his other patients, but he did for me. All that extra time, love, and care just for me. To this day, it chokes me up to think about the support staff and all the therapists who have believed in me. I am very grateful. I still carry all of it with me, and I continue to push myself because I never want to let him down.

LEARNING TO TALK

The speech pathologist was supposed to bring me a cap to put on my tracheotomy. It was such a small thing, but it was so important to help push the air up through my vocal cords so I could learn how to talk again. I relied on my iPad for the longest time to communicate, but this was about to change. I couldn't wait any longer for my speech pathologist to bring me a cap, so I decided to start talking on my own without the aid of my tracheotomy cover. As I did when the doctor informed me of my prognosis the night I woke up. I surprised everyone, family, nurses, and doctors included. They weren't expecting to hear me speak. Apparently, I had enough force and volume that I could talk without the cap. What a big sigh of relief, not only for my family but also for myself, because they thought they'd never hear my voice again. And they thought if I ever made any words, it would sound jumbled, and I would have to find other ways to communicate. It was another monumental moment in the early stages of my recovery, check.

LEARNING TO EAT

When my tracheotomy finally got removed and closed, I was able to have my first real, solid food. Eating was one of those things I easily took for granted, and I forgot how amazing it is to have the ability to chew and swallow food. It's incredible. The first thing I did when the doctor told me I was cleared to eat solid foods was order pizza. I ordered a combination pizza, like onions, with all the fixings on it. It came directly to the hospital, and I ate it with my family. I was on a phone call with Krista and her Uncle Jack. We talked about having beer and how much fun we would have eating and drinking together. While talking and laughing, an onion got lodged and stuck in my cheek.

I couldn't feel it. I couldn't even move the side of my face well enough to notice it was there. But then I tasted it on my tongue and immediately started vomiting. It was not the monumental first meal I was hoping for! Unfortunately, throwing up was a common occurrence at Walter Reed. I was used to it. The combination of the swelling in my brain, the medication, and having my tracheotomy cleaned on a regular basis meant I was throwing up a lot. It was just part of the fun. Whenever I think of beer and onions, I think about eating pizza at Walter Reed. It was part of my journey, and just trying to learn how to eat again.

FLIGHT TO CALIFORNIA

I was finally cleared to leave Walter Reed. Now that I was out of a coma, I didn't need that kind of intensive care. I was working on my recovery. The military gave me two hospital options: I could go to San Antonio, Texas, or Palo Alto, California; both hospitals specialized in polytrauma and helping people recover from brain injuries. Since I'm originally from Sacramento, California, Elk Grove, I picked Palo Alto. It made sense. My family would be closer, only two and a half hours away. So, California it was, and I would spend over a year in that hospital's inpatient program.

The next big step in my recovery was getting loaded onto a C130 bound for California. I was on an elevated gurney with multiple patients on board for the flight, which was a problem for the moment I needed to use the restroom. Thankfully, Chief Warrant Officer Brian Golik was there. He was my chaperone from EODMU1. I don't know how he felt about the whole situation, but I thought it was funny. I like teasing my old boss about the time when I couldn't walk and needed a lot of help getting around. The plane had bunk bed-style medical beds. And I was flying with other military medical patients and military equipment.

The whole flight was a nightmare. My catheter was out for a short while, and emptying my bladder was hard. I kept feeling an intense sensation, thinking I had to go all the time. About every 5-10 minutes, I'd ask for Chief Warrant Officer Brian Golik's help. Like a champ, he would pick me up off my medical bed and carry me to the bathroom. I probably asked him to help me at least twenty-five times. He'd get me to the bathroom; I'd sit down with the door wide open because I needed a way to let him know when I was ready for his help to get back to my medical bed. Every time, he would have to help me get my pants back on, pick me up, and carry me back to the bed and then back to the bathroom over and over again. We laugh about it now. But at the time, it was frustrating. It went on throughout the whole flight. I can still hear myself now. I'd say, "Hey Brian, my bad. I'm about to pee my pants. I need you to help me out again." Back and forth, we went, and nothing helped. If that's not embarrassing enough, I ended up getting air sick and throwing up all over the place, making for one miserable, long, solid flight across the states from DC, Maryland, to California.

GETTING A WHEELCHAIR

I regained my independence in Palo Alto, California. The doctors issued me a wheelchair, which was yet again another thing I had to learn to gain mobility. First, I figured out how to push the left wheel forward using my left arm. You think I'd be like Nemo, swimming around in a circle, going nowhere since I could only use one arm, but eventually, I got the hang of it. With time, I figured it out. I outsmarted the wheelchair and built enough strength into my left leg to start moving. I jimmied it up, taking the left leg rest off so I could get a better grip using my leg to steer. With my left leg pushing side to side and my left arm pushing the left wheel, I had power! As I got stronger and more independent with the aid of a cane, I was walking on my own. It was ugly and difficult, but once I was out of the wheelchair, I promised myself if I was able, I wouldn't use a wheelchair again. I remember the doctor saying, "You'll never walk again," and smiling as I walked again!

SPRINKLES CUPCAKES

I was posted up at the VA Medical Center. My sense of taste was returning. Food and flavors were becoming intense. Every Friday, someone would bring a couple dozen cupcakes for us inpatients from Sprinkles Cupcakes. They brought all the good ones, like red velvet with buttercream frosting, my favorite. They were just waiting in the reception area down the hall from my hospital room. The nursing staff would see me come out of my room, wheeling down the hall, determined, and on my way to get a cupcake. We'd pass smiles at each other and sometimes jokes. I'd poke fun at myself. Nothing too serious. Just jokes about how I would get fat from sitting around and eating cupcakes every week. And how maybe they should be motivating me to get out and about and socialize with something a little healthier and better for me. But really, it was the motivation I needed to not sit around watching TV, alone in my room, feeling so mopey about everything. I looked forward to Fridays and those little things in life, like a good cupcake. Nothing tasted better to me. It was magical. And to this day, Sprinkles Cupcakes brings me back to those days, those memories of recovering and being happy to be alive.

KEITH AND PACO AND BURRITOS

My mom's cousin Keith lived in Santa Cruz, only about forty-five minutes from the Palo Alto hospital where I stayed. He came to see me at least three times a week while I lived there. Every time, he would come with his friend Paco. They were both retired pilots for the Marine Corps in the Navy, respectively, so they understood a little bit about the culture, where I was coming from, the VA system, and how all that stuff works. But again, we would cause problems the whole time and cause trouble for the staff because, like we do, we tend to do things our own way. It was fun to build this relationship with this family member that I didn't even realize I had until he came to visit. We developed a friendship that I still cherish to this day. Keith and Paco going out of their way to hang out with me did so much more for me than I could notice then. Sometimes, it takes time to pass to be able to understand the benefits you get from things you've been through. Keith and Paco would always bring a new type of Mexican food burrito from a local Mexican food place next to the hospital, Santa Cruz, or wherever they were coming from. So, this became routine: every time they came in with a new burrito from a new place, I would become a food critic and chop it up with them, just hanging out and having fun.

One of the awesome things I got to do with Keith was once he signed me out of the hospital so that I could leave with him. I got to stay at his Santa Cruz house, which was so amazing. It was a beautiful home up in the mountains overlooking Santa Cruz. His wife Kathleen was an amazing cook. After dinner, we had a glass of wine, which I wasn't supposed to have. I slept in a real bed outside of a hospital. The next morning, we woke up early and went quail hunting. I was so grateful for Keith because he got me outside in nature again, which felt incredible. When we got back to the hospital, and they found out that I had gone hunting, they were extremely upset, and I got my privileges to leave taken away from me for a while. It was worth it, though, because it showed me that I could still do the things I wanted to do, thanks to Keith.

PHYSICAL THERAPY

Jen was my physical therapist at the VA Medical Center in Palo Alto. She was awesome. We had this kind of relationship where she would joke around, and we'd banter. She would poke fun at me, and I'd poke fun at her. It was the kind of dynamic I needed. Instead of feeling sorry for me, I needed someone to coach me and push me to improve.

She would bring a wooden block to our therapy sessions. The block had a belt strapped to it so she could put it around my waist and hold onto me so I wouldn't fall. I would step up and down on this stupid wooden block. It was maybe four or five inches high. I thought, "Climbing any set of stairs would have been a challenge and something I could get behind. But no, I was stuck with Jen and this stupid wooden block."

I would joke around and say to Jen, "Whenever I leave this place, I'm going to throw that block into a fire." The whole exercise was incredibly difficult, and I hated it. Somedays, I'd tell Jen that I was done with it. I didn't want to do it anymore. And she would say, "Well, that's too bad. Do it anyway." The more sets I did, the more depressing it became. Sometimes, after our sessions together, I'd get back to my room, and I would think, "How is this possible? How is this former athlete, this person who was one of the top-ranked hurdlers in California, struggling to step on a block of wood? It was frustrating. I did the work anyway.

MY PROSTHETIC LEG

The first thing people notice about me is my prosthetic leg. When I explain to them that I was shot in the head, it doesn't usually translate. They don't get it. They say, "Why did you lose your leg if you were shot in the head?" It's a long story. I point to my head and say, "The bullet wound that I took to my head paralyzed my right leg and right arm."

At first, the doctors gave me leg braces to wear. I hated them. They were ugly and bulky and didn't fit into my shoes. I had friends, military guys, who I knew lost a leg or two, and they were getting around better than me, and I had two legs! So, the fact that these guys had better mobility and were easily getting around pissed me off. I started talking to the doctors about it, and they thought I was acting crazy about the whole thing. But to me, it wasn't crazy. I had grander ideas. Things that I wanted to be able to do in my life. Activities that maybe these doctors didn't see coming. I still have the idea that someday, I'll be able to run again. So, they gave me some options. One of them was to fuse my ankles together. But that would have left me with limitations with the types of activities I was planning on doing. If I fused together my ankle, snowboarding would never be possible. It wouldn't even be something I could work my way up to. And running would be entirely off-limits.

After speaking with the doctors, my psychologists, and experts, I finally got the green light to talk to some surgeons to hear their opinions. I wanted to know if it was possible to amputate my leg. I had what is called a flail limb, or in other words, my leg no longer functioned. It was completely useless, even though my body was still pumping blood to my extremities. Amputating the flail limb was justified because, obviously, it was causing me problems and impacting my quality of life. And it's not like the surgery was uncommon. People voluntarily amputate their legs due to paralysis.

By amputating my right leg, I could start to imagine all the things I could do with my life. I could dream about running again. I decided I didn't want to be immobile. I was excited about the surgery. I spent hours looking on my phone for prosthetic legs. I thought they looked cool.

On January 5, 2016, I had my leg amputated at the UCLA Medical Center, thanks to a foundation called Operation Mend; they treat veterans' casualties of war with reconstructive surgeries, amputations, and really anything dramatic like the surgery I had, which amputated my right leg, just below the knee.

Weeks after my surgery, I was back home in Elk Grove, California, just in absolute miserable pain. I didn't sleep for three weeks. And then I finally called it. I flew back to UCLA to meet with my doctor. I couldn't take the pain anymore. I was experiencing what they call phantom pain. And nothing I had gone through, not even waking up from a coma or the pain of my traumatic brain injury and being shot, nothing compared to the phantom pain of my amputation. Being without a limb hurt, and it was bizarre. I couldn't even put a pack of ice on it to make it feel better.

This was all mental. It was a mental game of trying to convince my brain that nothing was there. Before I had my surgery, I couldn't feel a thing. My leg, my foot, it was all fine. But afterward, I could tell you exactly which toe was hurting and which was being pulled, broken, or crushed. It felt like someone was trying to pull my toes off on purpose.

I felt suicidal. I couldn't take it anymore. My body and my mind couldn't keep up the fight. And for the first time, I broke down in the doctor's office and allowed myself to cry. I let out every kind of emotion that I was feeling. I finally came to grips and let myself grieve. It was all of it. All the pain from everything I had gone through. It took everything out of me. I don't usually talk too much about my emotions. I don't wear them on my sleeve, but I had a total breakdown that day.

In that doctor's office, we discussed putting a permanent epidural into my back that would drip pain medication throughout the day. That was just one of the options that we discussed. But in the meantime, while I was thinking it over, they decided to give me morphine, 30 milligrams of morphine three times a day. Finally, I was relieved of the phantom pain. That night, I stayed at a hotel in L.A. I took it, and I slept so good. It was the best sleep that I had ever had. I spent the next five months on 90 milligrams of morphine, high as a kite, and barely surviving.

I could sense that I was getting addicted to it. I craved it. I wanted more even when I had already taken it. I was terrified. Addiction runs in my family, and this feeling of being addicted scared me. I didn't want to be an absent father. My wife, Sarah, was pregnant with our daughter, Tenley. So, I tried going off it cold turkey, but that was a terrible choice. The pain was still there. To get off it, I had to go through a full-blown opiate heroin withdrawal. I talked to my sister; fortunately, she is an M.D. She reinforced how it would be difficult to go cold turkey, especially from such a strong medication like morphine. And she also mentioned that it would also be dangerous and could create more medical difficulties, if not kill me.

I listened to her advice. I tapered down and went from 90 milligrams three times a day to 10 milligrams three times a day and eventually to zero. It took a total of six months to wean myself off that medication. I'm proud of myself. It was a good choice, and I'm happy I did it. To be present for my family means everything to me. I learned how to lean into pain and embrace it. I'm still here to feel it. The pain has taught me a whole new mindset of how to appreciate and deal with it. As difficult as it was to get my leg amputated, it would have been more challenging to sit back and watch other people live. Yeah, I've had to learn to walk again on a prosthetic, but it's been worth it. In

2022, I spent a week in Aspen at a winter sports clinic for disabled vets. And I've challenged myself to learn how to snowboard just like I said I would. Running is next.

ROBOTIC ARM

I was one of the first patients at Palo Alto to test out a robotic arm. It was called the Myomo. Everyone was excited to see how it was going to help me. The nurses hooked me up to sensors placed on my right bicep and tricep, so Myomo could read my muscular movement and help me try to activate my muscle memory. When they strapped me into Myomo for the first time, I kept thinking, "This is going to be a big disappointment." Because all the attempts I had made to move my arm before working with Myomo had failed. I was frustrated. I was struggling mentally. I had tried moving my arm with other therapies, and nothing had worked, which led to emotional lows. It was mentally difficult to put myself into a situation where I knew, potentially, it wouldn't work out. I had already dealt with so much disappointment that I was nervous to be let down again.

My therapists didn't allow me to give up. They kept pushing me to be stronger and encouraging me to do more. So, there I was, strapped into this device, sitting in the physical therapist's office, doing my best to have a good attitude about the whole thing. Everyone was huddled around to see what was going to happen. The therapist held my left hand. I squeezed and pulled against his palm to gain momentum in my mind, reminding my brain, "This is what it feels like to flex a bicep now. Let's do it with my right arm." The hope was that my brain would get the signal, firing through my left arm to my spinal cord and all throughout my nervous system and that it would be enough to activate the nerves that controlled the functioning and movement of my right arm, giving my right arm the ability to move.

I kept an eye on the screen of the handheld device that my therapist was holding. He pointed and said, "See there, that was a signal." Even though the signals were micro, something was happening. And that was enough for me to believe that the part of my brain that I thought was dormant was still active and could be strengthened. I tried to curl my arm, but nothing. Then he said, "Why don't you just try yawning." So, I yawned and pulled hard on his hand, and sure enough, my right bicep got the signal, and with a little aid to my elbow, my right arm curled. My mind was blown. "I had just flexed my bicep!" From then on, I started to wonder what else I could do. It became like a game.

MAGNET HEAD

The bullet hit me just above the left eyebrow and wrapped around my head, shattering almost the entire left side of my skull. The common practice with these types of brain injuries is to give the brain room to swell. They remove a large piece of the skull and preserve it under the skin on your abdomen or hip, so when the brain heals, they can replace the part they removed, which makes it a perfect fit. But I didn't have that opportunity because the bullet had shattered that area of my skull. I was forced to wear a helmet because half my skull was missing, making me look like an alien when I wasn't wearing it. I hated how dumb the helmet was and how it looked. It was all medical standard white and ugly. Somehow, my military team found out how much I hated it and hired a professional artist to custom paint it for me with an American flag, helicopters, and other cool guy stuff. After about seven months of wearing the helmet, the Palo Alto VA, in partnership with Stanford Medical, used CT scans and MRIs to build a 3D model of my skull to build a titanium plate that would fit perfectly to make my head round again.

After building the plate, they cut the left side of my head open, installed it, and sealed me up with over a hundred staples. I didn't have to wear the helmet anymore because now my skull had been replaced with a titanium plate, and I had the scar to prove it. Instead of looking like an alien with missing half of my skull, I looked more like an average person with a head again. That explains the big scar on the side of my head. It's not from the bullet. It's from the surgeries I had to replace my skull. I'm proud of that scar. I like to keep my hair short so people can see it. Trust me, you can't believe how disappointed I was when I found out that titanium was non-magnetic. When I first thought about having a metal plate in my head, I was like, "Oh, I could stick magnets on it!" I'll have the coolest Halloween costumes ever because I could stick things to my head, but to my disappointment, titanium turns out to be a non-magnetic metal. Oh well.

PARTY BOY

Once I got to the point as an inpatient at Palo Alto that I no longer needed 24-hour care, I was able to move into a more residential type of living situation while still an inpatient at the Palo Alto Hospital. It felt like a college campus, and I felt like a college student living in the dorm. I had my own room with a roommate, and there was a nursing staff there, but I did my own thing. I had a lot more freedom and free reign to do as I wanted. I ate what

I wanted to. I had to maintain and manage my schedule, which included all the therapies I had to go to and appointments I had to get to. It was up to me to get to them on time on my own. It was a transition and progression to being independent, to being on my own again.

They were teaching me how to cook and do my laundry. Learning these things a second time later in life may sound simple and easy, but it was extremely difficult and challenging. I continued to push my progression like I always do while still being stubborn 'ole Jordan, doing it my way, how I wanted to do it. It was the only way I knew how to push the lines of what I was allowed to do and what I should do as often and as frequently as possible. For example, I'm not a smoker. I've never been a smoker, but me and my roommate, Terrence Clark, would leave the confines of our floor and go outside and smoke cigarettes and talk trash to each other. It was a totally teenage rebellion type of thing.

We did anything to feel alive and somewhat normal. We wanted to be just two guys hanging out. Instead of two patients at a hospital, they didn't want to be at. He was a great roommate. We had names for each other; he was Tony Stark, and I was Superman Stevenson. In rebellion of the hospital food, we would order Domino's pizza whenever we could. We were getting it 3-4 times a week.

We would order pizza for the rest of the patients on our floor, hang out, and have pizza. It reminded me of what it felt like to hang with my buddies as a kid. Having something to look forward to again was nice because I had forgotten what that felt like. My need for adventure wore out my welcome at Palo Alto. Eventually, I was moved to San Diego as an inpatient at Balboa Medical Center. While in San Diego, I waited for my medical retirement paperwork to go through. I was progressing and soon would join the ranks of civilian life.

MOVING IN WITH MOM & DAD

After officially retiring and leaving the Balboa Medical Center, I moved in with my mom and dad. The career and plan I had set out to do for the rest of my life was over. I found myself in the middle of a divorce with my wife, Krista, who would soon become my ex. With limited ability to care for me and my son, I had no other option but to move back to my hometown and back into my father's place. I thought that part of my life (living with my parents) was over.

Krista and I had our son a few years before I was deployed. He was only two years old when I got shot. I had fears about being a dad before he was born. I wasn't ready to become a father. I was worried my son would grow to be embarrassed of me. That became my biggest fear. How would I be able to do all the things I wanted to do with him? How was I going to take care of him? I wanted to be a war hero. I wanted my son to see my strengths, not some wounded, weak guy. I was afraid. I was concerned that I wouldn't be able to be a good dad. Life, as we knew it, changed.

Moving home took a toll on me mentally. Even though I was with my parents, I was on my own and going through emotional ups and downs. I no longer had the support from the hospital inpatient facilities, and the staff I had leaned on wasn't around to keep me motivated. After five years of marriage and seven years with my military and medical team by my side, I was alone, with no one to hold me accountable. It was on me to push myself to pursue my own physical and mental recovery.

Being at home reminds anyone about who they are, where they come from, and all the things (good or bad) about their past. I was constantly reminded of who I used to be before my injuries. I hid my depression from my family and friends, putting on a mask to prove how strong I could be. The quiet moments when I was home alone haunted me. I was failing as a father and neglecting my friendships. I was lonely. I wanted to be in a romantic relationship, but I was failing at that, too. The thought of it all weighed on me.

I desperately tried to hang on, looking for a way to be the person I knew I was before my injuries. I looked for myself in bottles of liquor and meaningless hookups, all the stuff I had chased before. I was successful in creating destruction with behavior that led me to feel alone in my misery. I was familiar with this state of being. The hospital had me on suicidal watch several times before, so I was aware of myself and what could happen if I let it go too far. I wasn't ready to let go of who I used to be, but I needed to get a grip.

The guy I used to be was gone. I couldn't believe how I had spent 26 years becoming "Jordan," getting strong so I could be "Jordan." Before getting shot, I was in the best shape of my life. I kept thinking, "All that work is gone." He was never coming back. I kept comparing myself to the past, looking at myself in the mirror and trying to face reality.

I thought about my son. I thought about the father I could become. My dad always said, "I'm proud to be your dad." And I would say, "I'm proud to be your son." That's the way we express ourselves. That's how we said, "I love you." I thought about that. That was the kind of relationship I wanted to have with my son. I was willing to do whatever it would take to have that bond between us. Accepting what needed to change wasn't going to be easy. The bullet had killed me- Jordan 1.0. My life was never going to be the same. I was in a state of grief, mourning everything I loved and missed about myself and the stuff I enjoyed doing before I was injured.

ACCEPTANCE

Even during the period of loneliness, I felt there were glimmers of hope that kept me from following through on the desire to quit and kill myself. I adjusted, trying to do the best I could with the situation I was presented with. I began to rethink my values, principles, goals, and reasons for being alive. I wanted to live. I wanted to work hard. I wanted new reasons to push through the discomfort. I allowed myself to mourn the loss of who I was because the "old" Jordan was gone. I was never going to be able to be him again. The things I cared about started to change as I let go of what happened before I was hurt. I started embracing the new me and all the potential in front of me.

What could this 2.0 version of Jordan do now? My life could change. I thought about the lateral move I could make. What could I do with my life? The more I thought about my future, the easier it became to change my mindset. I let go of what was out of my control. I started to see what was important and what I would have to value about myself if I wanted to stay alive.

My life was still important. The more I reinforced that thought in my mind, the more I started to come out of the dark place I had been in for months. I recognized that I had been in a setback. I never anticipated or expected that this was what my life would be. Being honest with myself carried me through.

SMALL VICTORY

I decided to continue pursuing my passion and love for physical challenges. While living with my dad, the VA purchased me a recumbent bike. I decided I wanted to feel tall and get on two wheels again. I was determined to learn how to ride a bike. The recumbent bike only lasted so long before I started to get ideas of what I could do to *really* challenge myself. My dad's bike stared at me in his garage. This was precisely the type of fun I needed. I decided to clip my feet onto his bike without telling anyone one day. I then taped my right hand to the handlebar, hung onto the garage door with my left arm, and pushed myself down the driveway. I managed to make it around the block before I realized I didn't plan far enough ahead to figure out how to get off the bike if I was successful, so I crashed into our front yard lawn.

A LOVE STORY

Facing who I used to be, or what we can call Jordan 1.0, was one of the darkest times of my life. Once I fully accepted that I would never be him again, it made it easier to start working on who I would become in the future. That is when I began to come through the darkness. I realized this was an opportunity to recreate myself. I made a lateral movement away from who I used to be and started doing things differently. The more I accepted myself, the easier it was for others to accept me and show that they cared about me. It wasn't until I was on my own without support that I truly understood the power of a strong support system. There was no way I could do the things I was facing alone. It was a slow process, but I knew I was making progress when I started to have urges to start dating again. I was ready to move on from meaningless hookups and wanted something more.

I had grown up around the church, but it was never a big part of my life. As a youth in church, I looked up to Henry. He was the one who baptized me and had always been a staple of support for my family, especially when I was a kid. Henry dropped by one day to pay me a visit, and the very next day, Kent, another man from church, came to see me, too. To this day, they swear there was no coordination in their effort to bring me to church, but now, looking back, they obviously had a plan all along. Kent was not as subtle as Henry and got straight to the point by asking when I was coming back to church and if I needed a ride. It sounded interesting, so I took him up on the offer.

My town is the type of town where everybody knows everybody. So, when this beautiful woman I did not recognize approached us and said hi, my heart skipped a beat. When she introduced herself as Sarah Crandall, it clicked because I had gone to high school with her sister Heather and brother Scott, and we were all five years older than her, so it made sense why I didn't know her back then. To me, she was just Scott's little sister. But now, it felt like I was meeting her for the first time. It made sense why we hadn't crossed paths sooner because the whole time since I had moved back, she had been gone on a church mission. After we met at church that day, all I could think about was how pretty and nice she was. When I got home that evening, I looked her up online, found her on social media, reached out to her again to tell her how nice it was to meet her, and started pursuing her from there.

When I had the time to process meeting Sarah at church, I remembered I had asked her sister Heather a while back, when I moved back to Elk Grove after retiring from the military, if she knew any good girls she could introduce me to, and she said "no." As I thought about this, I realized that the only Jordan she knew was me from high school. So, it made sense why she wouldn't want her sister to date me. I wouldn't let her date old Jordan if she was my sister. I had to find a way to show her family that I was not that person anymore. So, I was all over it when they invited me and my son, Kayden, to go trick-or-treating on Halloween.

That was the night we connected, and it led to me asking her on our official first date. Until now, she was still feeling me out, trying to see if I would be a real fit for something serious. She wondered if I was a bad boy with tattoos and covering up an ugly face with my full beard. That's why she didn't hesitate to tell me that she thought I would look better clean-shaven. I suppose I didn't fit the mold she had in her mind of her dream husband.

The night before our first date, I decided to shave it all off to impress her. I was serious about dating her. She was right. I looked good. And she loved it. When I was first getting to know her, I couldn't help but tell her how beautiful she was all the time, and I still do. I couldn't believe how kind and loving she was to everyone around her. We're opposite in many ways. I'm more reserved, quiet, and content, and she's very vibrant, loud, outgoing, and loveable, the type of lovable you can't help but love. Whereas with me, you either love or hate me, and I'm okay with that. Something about us worked even though we were coming from different places. She was devout to the church, and I was covered in tattoos. She had never been married, and I had been divorced with a kid. Opposites truly do attract.

For our first date, I took her to the most romantic place I could think of, the gun range, of course!

But first, we stopped for sushi because we both love sushi. I was trying to impress her, so I took her to the best sushi restaurant in town. The date was a huge success. Sarah had never been introduced to guns before. I couldn't believe it! She completely embraced it and had a lot of fun doing it, which made me happy. I started to think we might be starting something awesome. I especially enjoyed sharing with her something that I enjoyed and something we could cherish as a bonding experience.

My neuropsychologist, Dr. Sarah Jackson, mentored and advised me when I was dating Sarah. I wanted to marry her. I brought my concerns to Dr. Jackson. I was constantly wondering how it was going to work out with Sarah. Dr. Jackson said, "How did it work out with other girls?" "Not so well." She said, "Maybe that's the point. Maybe what you've been looking for isn't what you need." A lightbulb went off. Maybe she was right.

Dr. Jackson suggested I bring Sarah to one of my appointments to learn about my condition and how it would affect my life moving forward. As our relationship evolved and got more serious, I wanted to make sure she knew about my symptoms and what my day-to-day life would look like for the rest of my life. I wanted to make her my wife, so it was a good idea to see where she was at with all of it. So, I set up the meeting. The first thing Dr. Jackson said was, "The odds of Jordan surviving and recovering the way that he has is as if you went to the beach, picked up a single grain of sand, and then put it back, left to go home, and then if you were to come back the next day and pick up the EXACT same grain of sand you picked up the day before."

Somehow, Jordan was able to survive and overcome everything he was faced with. Defying all odds. She explained that I needed someone to hold the flashlight and point it ahead to show me what I could do even when I couldn't see it yet. Sarah took pride in not letting me give up or start looking down on my situation. She found great purpose in that and accepted that role with love in her heart, and that was the moment we realized that we were meant for each other.

PART FOUR
JORDAN 2.0

A NOTE TO NURSES AND DOCTORS

I remember the doctors and nurses telling me I would never walk again when I was out of my coma. Hearing those words was painful for me, but at the same time, they were also very motivating. They made me angry and created this deep internal belief that I could get better so I could prove them wrong. I understand how important it is from a doctor's perspective to not give patients false hope. But at the same time, hope is what people need. When you use words like "never," you may not realize the severity of what you say and the absolute statement that you sear into your patient's mind. Your place of authority gives you power, and people listen. Your patients internalize what you say. Give people hope; don't take it away.

Unfortunately, too many people commit suicide. People like my friends. And maybe they gave up because they couldn't see their way out. Maybe they couldn't see a path of what they could do to recover. I'm not saying to give people false hope. I'm not even saying that it's your fault. I am saying how important it is to understand that your words have power and influence.

Sure, someone like me, in your eyes, may "never" be able to walk again. BUT. If you add the word "BUT." "BUT" changes everything. "BUT" is the hope people need. "You may not be able to walk again, BUT if you work hard and push yourself through the difficulties and challenges, that change puts the control we've lost back in our hands, so there is a chance that you can recover and get better. That little change, using the word "BUT," has the power to completely change how someone believes in themselves and how they view their diagnosis. "BUT" has the power to completely change someone's world.

MOTIVATIONAL SPEAKER

When I was living in Elk Grove, California, I was looking for an opportunity to work. I got a job with ISSE, monitoring the Air Force's nuclear launch facilities. As an EOD Technician, I had already received top security clearance, so it seemed like it would be a good fit. Coming from my background of disarming bombs, shooting guns, and jumping out of planes, to then sitting behind a desk watching facilities where bombs were being launched became boring fast.

About a year later, I left and began coaching high school sports. I loved coaching and seeing young people pursuing the same aspirations and dreams I had when I was their age in track and field. I realized building relationships with people was something that I enjoy. I remember my coaches that I had when I was young. I decided I wanted to be an example like my coaches were to me. Plus, I was good at it. Coaching high school students led to public speaking. And thanks to a friend of mine, Kevin Spies, who encouraged me to become a public speaker, I landed my first public speaking gig at the Rotary Club in Elk Grove. The first time I spoke, I felt that adrenaline rush I had been missing. I've found that speaking in front of a crowd has been the closest thing I can get to in terms of jumping out of planes and disarming bombs. As a bonus, I get to create relationships and help people with whatever they're going through.

CAR RACING

Once my mental health started improving, I was able to reintegrate myself into society. I decided to connect with veteran and military nonprofits, which gave me opportunities to do things and start living my life again. I've had some of the best experiences with Ranger Road. When I initially connected with them, I participated in a spartan race in the pouring rain with a couple other disabled veterans. I never thought I'd do anything like that again. I surprised myself, going through all the obstacles, hunting, cycling, picking up and carrying stones, the whole time pulling my friend through the course in his wheelchair and making it to the finish line. These events opened my eyes and helped me see how I could continue to be part of the team, helping my fellow veterans- guys going through similar things that I have gone through and still going through.

I realized I could be a louder voice and a positive influence for myself and others. My involvement in nonprofits like Ranger Road opened doors for me that I didn't think existed. I didn't know I could find so much joy in life and accomplish things I didn't think I'd be able to ever do again. One day, I was talking to Mikhail Venikov, the CEO and Founder of Ranger Road, and gave him the idea of racing cars. The idea came to me as an alternative option to skydiving. Usually, Ranger Road takes disabled vets skydiving in Davis, California. But with my experience with skydiving and my refusal to tandem jump, I needed a different kind of adrenaline rush. I could drive. From that conversation, Ranger Road Motors was born. With the help of donors, we started a racing team and events like *Gambler 500* and *24 Hours of Lemons*.

24 Hours of Lemons was the pinnacle. We took Volkswagen GTIs and custom-built them for disabled veterans to drive, with hand controls and everything you can imagine. We'd race around the track at over a hundred miles an hour, racing fifty to one hundred cars in every race. One day, Jay Leno happened to be filming for his show, *Jay Leno's Garage*, at one of the lemons races we were having at Sonoma Raceway in California. While filming an episode, one of their drivers ran into our driver and destroyed the back end of our GTI. After the race, Jay Leno came over, spoke to us, and invited us to be on his show. You can catch the episode of the fifth season, the episode titled "Tough Enough," where you'll see me and the rest of my racing team featured.

The best part is how Jay Leno made fun of me. I told him I got shot in the head, and he joked, "How it's a good thing I didn't have anything up there to get hurt." I could care less that I was the butt of Jay Leno's joke. This was Jay Leno, and a few years before, I was on the brink of giving up. I was back into society, doing things I had never done before and never thought would even be possible. Going that fast is such a thrill. I never thought I'd experience that kind of rush again. It's been an incredible experience to share it with other veterans who have felt the same way. I've since passed the torch, and now, Ranger Road continues to run the program. Still allowing other veterans to feel what I felt.

I'M PROUD TO BE YOUR SON, DAD

My son is always the first to tell people how his dad is a hero with a robotic leg. He has always thought of me as "cool." For his sixth-grade elementary school project at the celebrity wax museum, he got to pick someone he looked up to, and chose me. I was his school report! This was so awesome because not only was my son proud of me, but he told his classmates all about me and how he wanted to be just like me! He even shaved the shape of my scar into the side of his hairline so he could look just like me, and he does it every now and again just for fun.

LATERAL MOVEMENTS

I chase experiences. I don't like being stagnant. When I'm not going after a goal, I usually feel unhappy. So, having a goal mindset, to me, is progression. There is no finish line. Progression begets progression, a process of continual growth. There are a lot of things and people in this world who will tell you what will bring happiness, like making a million dollars. But then what? If you're chasing material items, you'll never find happiness. So, what I do instead is create movement in my life toward what I believe is my life's purpose.

I don't like end goals because people often overlook the things learned along the way. I've learned to appreciate the process, even the setbacks. And when there are setbacks, we don't give up. We keep going. Progression is a mindset that allows for lateral movement. I never want to stop growing and progressing. I try my best to keep moving forward and being a better version of myself than I was before. As humans, there's always progress to be made. There are ways to improve ourselves at whatever we're doing. I like the idea of lateral movement. Because what happens is when something is no longer achievable, instead of thinking there's only one way to achieve the goal, I think laterally, in other words, what are the ways around it?

You can go in a different direction. I look for ways around it and how I can laterally step. This mindset has benefited me and has helped me throughout my recovery. So often, people think they must progress in big ways. This isn't true. Progression happens in small increments, growing as a person in the little things, even with something as small as brushing your teeth. That seems like a little stupid thing, but my point is just because you brushed your teeth once doesn't mean you're good at it forever. Keep learning. Keep doing things. Don't chase singular things. Chase the idea of progression. For example, I really wanted to walk again. Sometimes people ask me, "How did you do it?" I visualized walking up to my son and picking him up again. Getting there started when I was able to stand up independently, then ended with finally being able to pick up my boy again. And once I did it, I didn't stop there. I asked myself, "What else can I do?" Just because I met my goal doesn't mean the learning stops there. There's always something, and I continue to learn and become a pro in progression. Being in that state of mind is where I find my happiness. In that pursuit, I've now been hiking and going on cross-country hunting road trips with my son.

YOU CAN TRY

Fortunately, I learned how to reframe my thought patterns. I ask myself, "What can I do." Emphasizing the can. I can drive. I can walk. I am a proud dad again. I'm a public speaker. I'm reaching out to people and trying to touch lives. Trying to help people like you realize just how much you can do if you allow yourself to get into the mindset of trying and saying, "I can."

So often, people get stuck on what they can't do. They can't get past the can't. They don't allow themselves to even see the opportunity for the "can." They think, "What if I can't do x,y,z." It always bothers me, and I think,

"Yeah, but what if you can?" You don't know until you try. Thinking "I can" thoughts allow for possibility and the chance to be successful. Things can get better. Given enough time, almost anything can improve. I wish and hope more people would give themselves the opportunity for things to get better. Give yourself a chance. Believe that it's possible. The truth is,

"Giving yourself the opportunity to try takes

you past the "I can't" and allows you to

find the "I can."

-Jordan Stevenson

ACKNOWLEDGMENTS

The Power Behind Unstoppable

This book is a trophy for the incredible things that are possible when humans help each other. Every breath I take serves as a reminder of the countless number of people who are responsible for me being able to still experience life. The level of help that I have received is at a magnitude that is truly unimaginable. I wouldn't dare attempt to thank everyone individually because, for every person I would list, there would be three more that I would be forgetting. Instead, to anyone who has contributed effort, big or small, in any way to my recovery, thank you. Thank you for walking with me. You and your compassion to help are the sole reason I have been able to triumph over some of the fiercest challenges a person can possibly face. I'm driven to prove your efforts were well-spent by continuing to push myself toward my maximum potential.

Thank you to my parents, Doug and Michelle. I am grateful for your unwavering support throughout my life. I am blessed to have had the support and love of you both with every endeavor I have chosen to pursue. You two are examples for me to live by, resemble, and pass on to my kids. I love you both, and I'm proud to be your son.

To Justin and Amber, my brother and sister: I will continue to look up to you two my entire life as your baby brother.

To the men and women I have had the honor to serve in both past and present, there are no words to explain the bonds we all share. You are all Giants among men!

And to my wife, Sarah Stevenson, I would be lost without your love and support.

To my children, everything I do is for you! I love you, and I'm proud to be your dad.

And to the entire team at Golden Lane Publishing, thank you for believing I could write this book. It wouldn't have been possible without your support and guidance. You said you could pull my stories out of my head and onto paper, and you did just that.

It's been challenging to find the words to adequately express my gratitude to everyone who has been involved in my healing journey. When the weight of my life has been too heavy, you have helped me carry the load. It is for you that I will press on and never lose hope!

ABOUT THE AUTHOR

Jordan Stevenson is a veteran, public speaker, coach for young adults, and a proud dad. He is a thriving example of what's possible even when up against insurmountable odds. His message of hope is a beacon for anyone who has faced adversity and has ever wondered if they would make it through. He lives in Spanish Fork, Utah, with his wife, Sarah, their three kids, and their growing family. He enjoys focusing his time in his community, coaching track and field, and being of service to his fellow veterans.

headshotjordan.com

 instagram.com/headshotjordan

Made in the USA
Middletown, DE
25 September 2023